Mary -

To beautiful homes
and interiors. Thank you
so much for trusting me
with yours.

xo Jackie S.

Segreto

SECRETS TO FINISHING BEAUTIFUL INTERIORS

Segreto

SECRETS TO FINISHING BEAUTIFUL INTERIORS

BY LESLIE SINCLAIR

Graphic Design and Layout - Muffy Buvens

Primary Photographer - Wade Blissard

"To achieve a sophisticated backdrop
for this formal living room, we applied
a glaze on the wood paneled walls,
bringing depth and interest to the room
through technique and the perfect
combination of colors."

- Leslie Sinclair

All finishes featured in *Segreto: Secrets to
Finishing Beautiful Interiors* are created by
Leslie Sinclair and applied by the *Segreto
Finishes* team.

First Limited Edition 6000 copies
© Copyright 2011 Segreto Publishing
Orders: 713-461-5210
info@segretofinishes.com

Graphic design and layout by Muffy Buvens
Photography credits and copyrights
on page 299
Printed and bound in China

Library of Congress Cataloging-in-
Publication Data
Sinclair, Leslie
Segreto: Secrets to Finishing Beautiful
Interiors/Leslie Sinclair. -1st ed.
ISBN 978-0-9833914-8-7

Designer - Julie Dodson
Builder - Epic Custom Homes

With much GRATITUDE

THANKS ARE EXTENDED TO ALL OF THE WONDERFUL homeowners, designers, builders and architects with whom I have worked over the years. It has been my honor to be involved with every project and my privilege to be allowed to create the beautiful backdrops that help make each of my clients' houses his or her own. Without their trust, I never would have been able to develop my passion for finishes into such a rewarding career.

Thank you to all of my staff - both past and present - who, through their dedication to superior craftsmanship and organization, have made Segreto Finishes a quality firm. Without each of you, I would not have been free to focus on the creative and design elements of my business.

Thanks to my wonderful husband, John, and our children, Matthew, Kirby and Sammy, who have been supportive from the beginning, tolerating my long hours, allowing people to see finishes in our home and pitching in to help whenever I have asked. Thanks to my parents who raised me to do my best, work hard and never give up on my dreams. I am grateful to Mom and Ken and appreciate their help and their attendance at every company party. Thanks to my friends who have always been happy to talk, even when longer periods than I would like pass between calls.

A special thanks goes to Muffy Buvens, Wade Blissard, Karen Donoghue and Nicole Jacobson. Without your long hours and dedication to this project, the book never would have been completed.

- Leslie Sinclair

Custom artwork by Leslie Sinclair from Segreto Studios.

Table OF CONTENTS

Designer - Tami Owen
Building Design - Robert Dame Design
Builder - Stonehenge Classic Homes, Inc.

Fine FINISHES
AN INTRODUCTION

THE WORLD OF DECORATIVE PAINTING IS LIMITLESS, EVER-changing and richly complex. Finishes for walls, ceilings, floors and cabinetry are crucial to the embodiment of a home's character. My niche in the world of design motivates me to constantly explore new techniques and finishes that complement a vast multitude of styles and personal tastes.

Working with designers, architects, builders and homeowners inspires me to interpret many beautiful ways to finish a home. My philosophy is that when you enter a room, your eyes should not be drawn to to any one element or finish, but instead, you should view the surroundings as a whole.

I aspire to create the perfect backdrop that enables fabrics, art and furniture to blend and establish a particular mood. A palette developed to complement your home's architecture and design can give your surroundings a completely new perspective.

Since *Segreto Finishes'* first endeavor over 16 years ago, I have been privileged to work in countless exquisite homes with many wonderful people. Although a picture really is worth a thousand words, I want to share some of my secrets on how to enhance your home by melding architecture, period and personal style with the perfect finish.

In the sections that follow, *Segreto: Secrets to Finishing Beautiful Interiors* discusses a variety of finishes. SECTION 1 explores plastered homes, presenting the different moods plaster evokes to suit an array of design styles. In SECTION 2, stencils, murals, faux finishes, cabinets and plaster are combined, revealing secrets behind mixing colors, designs and textures in a manner that still maintains continuity from room to room. SECTION 3 provides inspiration for kitchens and bathrooms with numerous examples of how to make finishes work in these spaces. SECTION 4 is a reference section containing samples of different finishing techniques and information on their historical application in home design. The book concludes with a resource directory featuring the designers, architects, builders and retailers that contributed to each home's interior.

My hope is that by looking at these beautiful interiors, you realize the impact that well-crafted finishes give to a home's over all character, and sense my joy in creating each finish.

Designer - Kara Childress
Architect - Newberry Campa Architects, LLC
Builder - Windham Builders

OF PLASTER

The quiet sophistication

THE FIRST SECTION OF *SEGRETO: SECRETS TO Finishing Beautiful Interiors* focuses on beautiful interiors of plastered homes, showcasing this product's ability to create depth and warmth in a space, while lending a quiet sophistication to a home's architecture, art and furnishings.

Historically known throughout the world for its beauty, subtlety and durability, the art of plaster is being revived. Believed to have originated in Mesopotamia before recorded history, plaster has been used to adorn the walls of architecture that has transformed our world for thousands of years. The Egyptians burned gypsum in open-air fires, crushed it into powder and mixed it with water to plaster ancient pyramids. Venetians also embraced plaster but added marble dust to the mixture, producing heavier variation and adding more sheen to the finish. In the frescoes of Michelangelo's celebrated Sistine Chapel, pigment was applied directly to wet plaster, taking months to dry but resulting in the magnificent murals that are still admired today.

By the 17th century, the plasterer's skills were crafted to a level unparalleled in history. Paris was the capital of plaster ("Plaster of Paris") due to large quarry deposits of gypsum located in Montmartre. Then, after the 1666 Great Fire of London devastated the city, King Charles II ordered that all wooden houses be covered with plaster to protect them against fire, spreading the prevalence of plaster across the continent. These gypsum plasters were a harder, faster drying material than the lime plasters used in ancient times.

Plaster over lath or wire mesh remained popular in the United States until sheetrock, less costly and easier to install, became available in the 1950s. The technique of plastering had all but fallen out of fashion until artisans found that it could be used as a veneer applied directly over sheetrock. With this new discovery, renewed appreciation for the once lost art form wove its way into the world of design once again.

The use of plaster in settings today creates stunning architectural effects. The depth and movement of this material, when applied over sheetrock, produces the impression of hand-carved archways and windows appearing to be placed in deep wall insets. The use of plaster allows door, window, crown and base moldings to be minimized, while still maintaining the design, thus offsetting the price of the product. Its character truly blends with any surrounding.

Veneer plaster, a technique that is versatile and less expensive than historical plastering methods, conveys the same grace, beauty and warmth when used in a home. Many modern variations of plaster are used today, including synthetic and natural products. In numerous instances, sheetrock mud that has been primed, painted and glazed is identified as plaster. Although all are beautiful options, natural plasters offer a depth and sophistication that cannot be duplicated.

"This project is where my love of plaster began.
Although I admitted that I had never plastered a
home, the homeowners took a leap of faith and
trusted that this finish would
create the established look they desired.
I am eternally grateful for their confidence in me.
This not only started a new division of my
company but spurred a trend in
Houston's wall finishes."
- L.S.

Texas
HILL
COUNTRY
REVIVED

Designer - Ginger Barber
Architect - Tom Wilson & Associates
Builder - Southampton Group

THE DESIGN CONCEPT OF THIS NEWLY CONSTRUCTED HOME revolves around the idea of combining two old stone farmhouses, stripping them to their shell and integrating more contemporary interior elements, melding the two together. The use of reclaimed beams, flooring and stone composes the renovated shell, while the steel casement windows, sleek cabinetry, contemporary art and eclectic furnishings modernize the space for a unique, Texas Hill Country look. Originally planning a faux paint treatment, the homeowners and design team decided instead to use pigmented gypsum plaster on the walls and ceilings to impart the substantiality, weight, integrity and thickness reminiscent of century-old Texas architecture like the Alamo.

Rug from Carol Piper Rugs. Bench from Watkins Culver Antiques.
Sconces from Formations. Stone from San Jacinto Stone.

REMOVING THE BASEBOARDS
and plastering down to the floor imparts continuity.

*Lighting from Watkins Culver Antiques. Chairs from
Cameron Collection. Artwork in dining room by Joe Andoe.*

"There is something about the way light reflects off plaster that not
only opens up a space, but also evokes serenity and warmth."

*Left: Artwork by Charles Thomas O'Neil. Above: Antique heart pine floors from Custom Floors Unlimited. Leather ottoman and chair from Shabby
Slips. Sofas and chairs from Cameron Collection. Artwork over sofa by Michel Alexis. Four piece artwork by Jackie Tileston. Etagere from Walkins
Culver Antiques.*

"When plastering the walls and ceilings of a newly constructed home, the sheetrock should be taped, floated and lightly sanded. There is no need to fix imperfections in the sheetrock or to texture, prime or paint the walls. This savings can offset the overall cost of applying plaster."

Fluently FRENCH

Designer ~ Cindy Witmer
Architectural Consultant ~ Sarah West
Building Design ~ Robert Dame Designs
Builder ~ Parker House Inc.

SHAKESPEARE WROTE THAT ART, IN ITSELF, IS nature. Subdued hints of color and texture carefully woven throughout this home's open floor plan bring a distinctive element to this French inspired home. The harmony of architectural antiquities, the warm influence of plaster on the walls and the fine finishing on cabinetry and beams conjure up the gentle notes of Provence that the homeowners sought.

Stone table from previous page and mantel from Chateau Domingue. Fixtures from Aquilla Little at Marburger Farm Antique Show. Chandelier and 19th c. French chairs from Tara Shaw, covered in Fortuny fabric. Custom daybed from Hien Lam Upholstery. Coffee table from Vieux Interiors. Clock from Angie Tyner at Marburger Farm Antique Show. Rug from Creative Flooring Resources. Wine rack from Joyce Horn Antiques.

25

THE PALETTE OF FABRICS

and the rich tones of the wood were the foundation upon which the paneling was aged and finished. By integrating the hues of the fabric wall covering, the subdued wash complements the colors of the room and enriches the knotty alder wood.

Left: Table and chairs from Joyce Horn Antiques. Antique French baker's rack from Chateau Domingue. Rug from Creative Flooring Resources. Chandelier from AREA. Above: Coffee table and artwork by Diana Hendrix from AREA. Light fixture from Brown. Custom barstools from Antiques at Dunlavy.

PLASTER AND CABINET FINISHES

marry all of the architectural elements in this kitchen, enhancing the character of the reclaimed brick and stone tiles on the backsplash and counters.

Reclaimed brick backsplash, iron fireback and stone counters from Chateau Domingue. Light fixture from Brown.

SUBDUED BLUE-GRAY PLASTER

brings sophistication to the 18th century stone sink and antique tile floor. The reclaimed door was enhanced by a series of washes.

Above: Sink from Chateau Domingue. Door from Joyce Horn Antiques. Antiqued mirror on door and walls from Frame Tek Art Services. Right, above: Chandelier and sconces from Aquilla Little at Marburger Farm Antique Show. Right, below: Chandelier from Tara Shaw. Flooring from Materials Marketing.

THE NEWLY HAND-HEWN

beams are aged and treated to add
character to the ceiling.

THE CALCUTTA-ORO

marble vanities mirror the movement of the
plaster blanketing the groin vaults.
A dry brush treatment on the cabinets
brings elegance to the space by
incorporating a bit of silver.

Gracefully ECLECTIC

Designer - Don Connelly
Architect - Michael T. Landrum Inc.
Builder - Corbel Custom Homes

THIS HOME GIVES BALANCE TO THE COMBINATION OF OLD and new, incorporating clean architectural lines, reclaimed materials and a deliberate mix of contemporary and antique furnishings and art. In this minimalistic approach to design, each individual piece is crucial to the room's overall success. The finishes follow suit by being simplistic and sophisticated - still making an impact without overwhelming the other elements. In spaces with negligible trim details, gypsum plastered walls and ceilings stand on their own, working as a perfect backdrop for an eclectic interior.

Artwork by Michelle Y. Williams. Antique flooring by Custom Floors Unlimited. Floor lamps by Michael Aram. Coffee table from AREA.
Fabric for slipper chairs from Lee Jofa. Custom ottoman fabric from George Cameron Nash. Rug from Creative Flooring Resources.

"Plastering these walls that were inspired by the designer's visit to an old European home provided another first for me."

ON THESE WALLS OF PECKY CYPRESS,

a thinned-down plaster exposes the texture and grain of the wood in a unique way. Wonderfully eclectic, the rustic nature of the walls balances the contemporary art and furnishings.

Artwork by Christina Karll.

To develop an old world, rubbed-back look, a textured plaster serves as the base for a pale blue and green stenciled pattern. Washing with a second layer of plaster creates a wonderful fresco appearance.

French COLONIAL

Designer - Sandy Lucas
Building Design - Robert Dame Designs
Builder - Mission Constructors, Inc.

THIS FUNCTIONAL, CREOLE-INSPIRED HOME SIMULATES the understated elegance and character of historical Louisiana architecture by A. Hays Town that the homeowners have long admired.

The house is filled with reclaimed materials such as 19th century French clay floor tiles, antique doors and light fixtures. The texture of the plastered walls gives dimension and depth to the spaces and successfully balances the weightiness of the knotty alder woodwork and antique finishes. All rooms graciously open to each other, and the large, multipurpose great room serves equally well for everyday living or for large-scale entertaining.

The design of the study replicates that of the famous Pigeonniers found at the Parlange Plantation, an estate owned by friends of the homeowners in New Roads, Louisiana.

Reclaimed hickory floors throughout from Custom Floors Unlimited. 18th c. painting "Rebekah and Eliezer at the Fountain" from Cavalier Fine Art.

"I have found that gypsum plasters work best in light to medium colors.
The product is not made to hold the pigments of darker tones."

FEATHERING PLASTER OVER
the openings of the formerly solid brick archways
creates a softer transition.

18th c. French limestone fireplace from Brian Stringer Antiques. Hearth from Chateau Domingue. Antique Serape rug from Matt Camron Rugs & Tapestries. 19th c. French oak harvest table from Watkins Culver Antiques. Chairs from Neal & Co. Upholstery.

Altered for

an aged look, the antique pillar legs ground the island and set the tone of this kitchen.

Island legs from Brown. Concrete tiles from Chateau Domingue. Barstool fabric from Perennials Outdoor Fabrics.

THE DOUBLE-SIDED FIREPLACE

with a raised hearth supplies
warmth and architectural
interest to both the master
bedroom and bathroom.
Applying the same plaster from
the walls over noncombustible
material allows the fireplace to
be a subtle focal point, blending
with the walls to create a
soothing architectural effect.

*Rug from Matt Camron Rugs & Tapestries.
Bench from Joyce Horn Antiques. Custom
headboard from Neal & Co. Upholstery.
Antique musical carving from Tara Shaw.*

HOUSTON'S
Honoring
HISTORY

Designer - Cathy Chapman
Architect - Shannon Sasser AIA
Renovator - Roy Pruden LLC

DESIGNED AND BUILT BY KATHERINE MOTT IN 1930, THIS Tudor style home remains on Houston's historical registry.

The original plastered walls brought textural interest and substantial depth to the space but were in need of repairs. To counter the effects of repeated paint jobs while still keeping the home's integrity intact, a gypsum-based finish coat, made of the same materials as the original plaster, was applied to the walls throughout the main areas.

By incorporating the modern technology of mixing pigment into plaster, the walls obtain a new dimension and beauty that painted plaster cannot achieve. The finished product enhances the home's woodwork, offering an understated elegance. The floors, honed to appear more subtle, also acquire a new twist.

Artwork over couch by Joseph Havel. Antique French stools and settee from The Gray Door.
Branch side table from Rose Tarlow Melrose House. Drop leaf table from Twenty Six Twenty.

DIFFERENT CEILING TREATMENTS give the living and dining rooms their own personality while still retaining continuity from space to space. Pulling shades of peach and coral from the rugs and fabrics onto the ceilings grants each room a sense of distinction.

Left: Oushak rug from Marc Anthony Rugs. Stone fireplace mantel designed by Chapman Design and fabricated by JVC Stoneworks. Mirrored sconces from Brown. Antique Italian cabinet from Watkins Culver Antiques. Silk fabric on draperies from Cowtan & Tout. Drapery trim from Bailey & Griffin.
Above: French chairs from Louis J. Solomon. Fabric on back of chairs from Silkworks. Oushak rug from Nouri Gallery. Artwork by Joseph Havel.

"Pulling the wall treatment onto the ceiling extends the room's lines, highlighting the shape of the room and enhancing the ceiling beam detail."

THIS DREAMY BEDROOM SUITE

radiates charm and comfort, as the plastered walls and
ceilings echo the fabric and tile colors.

Left: Master bathtub and tile floors from Waterworks. Chaise fabric from Bennison Fabrics. Stool fabric from Nancy Corzine. Oushak rug from Marc Anthony Rugs. Above: Custom bed designed by Chapman Design. Draperies made by Topstitch, Inc. Fabric from Silkworks.

SUBTLE *Sophistication*

Designer - Kara Childress
Original Architect - Eubanks Group Architects
Original Builder - Thompson Custom Homes

TO REFLECT THE SOPHISTICATED YET UNDERSTATED personality of the homeowners, layers of design elements, rugs and textures transform the space from very formal to elegantly casual. Plastering the walls and glazing the staircase balustrade warm up the room, giving the home instant age and character. The addition of a jute runner on the marble staircase and key antique light fixtures adds to the drama of an 18th century Flemish tapestry, softening the formality of the previous owners' design.

Jute runner from Creative Flooring Resources. Antique Flemish tapestry from Empire Antiques. Italian chandelier from AREA. Custom table skirt by Heine's Custom Draperies. Fabric from Groves Bros. Fabrics. Trim from Samuel & Sons. Sconces from Brown. French chair from Joyce Horn Antiques.

Walnut bench from Formations. Antique pillows from Watkins Culver Antiques. Custom draperies by Heine's Custom Draperies. French trumeau mirror from AREA. Antique faience jars and candelabras from Joyce Horn Antiques. Oushak rug from Creative Flooring Resources.

Above: Custom Florio Collection embroidered linen draperies by Heine's Custom Draperies. Dining table from Dennis & Leen. Custom antique iron balcony/console from Chateau Domingue. Italian oil painting from W. Gardner, Ltd. Antique Biot jar from Liz Spradling Antiques. Antique French trumeau mirror from Tara Shaw. Italian chandelier from Annette Schatte Antiques. Right: Custom dried arrangements from For All Occasions.

"I love the way plastered ceilings and walls add a sense of romance to evening entertaining."

Essence de Provence

Architectural Consultant - Sarah West
Architect - Architectural Solutions, Inc.
Builder - Richard Price Custom Homes

LIKE A PASSPORT TO ESCAPISM, THIS HOME INTEGRATES reclaimed architectural antiques with finishes in the manner of a Provencal landscape. Plaster weaves every room together, creating movement and harmony amongst the natural wood and antique stone used in the building process.

18th c. door from Chateau Domingue. Pottery from Joyce Horn Antiques and Chateau Domingue.

Light fixture from Joyce Horn Antiques.

"If creating an authentic
sense of yesteryear is one of the
goals in building a home, a
natural plaster product is
the best choice. It has the
advantage of giving credibility
to the walls just as the
use of reclaimed materials
contributes to the genuineness
of floors, beams and
other surfaces."

PLAYING OFF THE TEAL

embellishments in the antique French canvases,
the cool tones of the plaster lend coherence to
the textures in the dining room.

Antique panels from Chateau Domingue. Light fixture from AREA.

"The intricately carved moldings stand on their own. They were painted a color similar to the wall finish to highlight their details rather than a contrasting band that would divide the ceiling and the walls."

Neoclassical INFLUENCE

Designer - Cathy Carabello
Architect - Villa Residential Design
Builder - Michael Thurman Custom Homes

THIS PALLADIAN-INFLUENCED HOME MIXES TRADITIONAL and contemporary styles through the placement of antiques alongside new furniture and colorful abstract artwork. Layered with intricate architectural elements, the home required a finish to add warmth to the room and create a soft transition between the elaborate moldings, elegant marble and exquisitely designed staircase.

Maintaining the prevalence of these accents while tying them together, a smooth finish of tinted, hard troweled plaster creates a delicate sheen without the intense polish of Venetian plaster. The finished effect balances the room's design features and highlights its many surfaces. These finishes soften the space so the architecture and art remain the focus.

Artwork by Dick Wray. Furnishings from Vieux Interiors and AREA.
Custom chandelier from Alcon Lightcraft Co.

GROIN VAULTS ARE AREAS IN WHICH

many people choose to incorporate decorative painting techniques such as scrolls and embellishments. With soft marble surfaces and beautiful lighting, this space needs no other enhancements - plaster is sufficient ornamentation, as its chiseled appearance enhances the curves of the vaults.

Left: Custom chandelier from Alcon Lightcraft Co. Custom dining table from Custom Creations Furniture. Dining chairs and fabrics from David Sutherland Showroom.
Above: Custom lighting from Alcon Lightcraft Co. Bath hardware from Elegant Additions.

Warm & INVITING

Designer - Nicole Zarr
Building Design - Robert Dame Designs
Builder - Allan Edwards Builder

THIS HOME HAS A RICH, OLD WORLD AMBIANCE that makes each area feel warm and welcoming. The high ceilings in the foyer and living room entertain a majestic sense through the movement and grace of the plaster as it varies throughout. The abundance of natural light along with the soft glow from antique fixtures enhance the beauty of the natural plaster finish which graces these majestic spaces.

Writing table from Liz Spradling Antiques. Demilune from Kirby Antiques. Antique panels from 2 Lucy's.

"The gypsum based plasters of today offer some of the same insulating, noise canceling and fire retardant qualities of the original lath and plaster method."

Antique fragments from 2 Lucy's. Oval painting and settee from Liz Spradling Antiques. Coffee table and tea table from Joyce Horn Antiques. Painted tabouret from AREA.

THE EMBROIDERY

on the drapery inspired the color for this
room's plaster. To add more definition
to the ceiling, a custom design adorns
the corners of this inviting dining room.

*Light fixture from Tara Shaw. Table from Joyce
Horn Antiques. Chairs from The Gray Door.
18th c. armoire from The Mews.*

"The plaster in this wine room is troweled in a heavier manner, aging the
walls to enhance the rustic nature of the room."

Wine barrel ends and etabli from Joyce Horn Antiques. Table and chairs from Tara Shaw. Door fronts from Wirthmore Antiques. Floor from Chateau Domingue.

"Imagine tan painted walls, white casements going around the openings, narrow plank reddish hardwoods and a white painted wood balustrade staircase with a stained top. To transform this space, we chose neutral plaster to thread throughout the open floor plan."

A BIT OF *Provence*

Designer - Kara Childress
Builder - Goodchild Builders

AFTER SURVIVING WATER DAMAGE, THESE HOMEOWNERS decided to customize and renovate their traditional "spec" house. Plastered walls and ceilings, along with trim painted to match, flow from one space to the next, blending effortlessly with the new limestone floors and neutral fabrics. The subtle palette and warm plaster marry to create a calm and comfortable, yet elegant home. Wrought iron staircases add wonderful character to the home. A series of milk wash glazes on the metal balustrade lends an age-old flavor.

Antique French panels from Karla Katz Antiques. Demilunes and mirrors from AREA. Antique beams from The Woodshop of Texas.

Antique French herbier collection
from Joyce Horn Antiques. Artwork
from AREA. Reclaimed floors from
Custom Floors Unlimited.

ALTHOUGH THE KITCHEN CABINETS ARE ORIGINAL,

paint and glaze impart character, producing a furniture look and offering the space a Provencal feel.

Fireplace from Materials Marketing. Kitchen table from
Custom Floors Unlimited. Lantern, 19th c. tile backsplash and
17th c. stone counters from Chateau Domingue.

French SERENITY

Designer - Terry Harmon
Building Designer - Rodney Stevens
Builder - Barnett Custom Homes, Inc.

COMING FROM A TRADITIONAL GEORGIAN HOME FILLED WITH mahogany furnishings and vibrant colors, the homeowners gravitated toward a new style, culling inspiration from Belgian and Parisian books that feature sparse home designs and focus on beautiful walls and flooring. Soothing, neutral tones in a textured gypsum plaster mimic the walls of these understated interiors.

Left: Floors from Custom Floors Unlimited. New Zealand wool runner from M & M Carpet. Custom staircase railing from Metal Railing of America, Inc. 18th c. French chest from Shabby Slips. 18th c. Aubusson tapestry from Joyce Horn Antiques. Above: 19th c. enfilade trumeau and gilt Louis Philippe mirror from Joyce Horn Antiques. 19th c. Louis XVI chandelier from The Pittet Company. Chinoiserie patterned gaufrage velvet on dining chairs from Scalamandre.

19th c. French bergere and fauteuils from Joyce Horn Antiques. 18th c. French table from Le Louvre
French Antiques. Custom sofa from J. Roman Upholstery. Oushak rug from Creative Flooring Resources.

"An option for treating a ceiling in rooms that are plastered is to paint the ceilings the color of the trim. It offers a clean look, and unifies adjoining rooms whose walls are simply painted. Note in this home, however, it was crucial to plaster the entrance ceiling, since it wrapped underneath the staircase."

Drapery fabric and linen velvet on slipper chairs from Scalamandre. Cocktail table from Dennis & Leen. 18th c. French marble-topped chest and Italian candlesticks from Joyce Horn Antiques. 18th c. gilt mirrors from Legacy Antiques. Fireplace screen from Lamani Designs. Oushak rug from Carol Piper Rugs

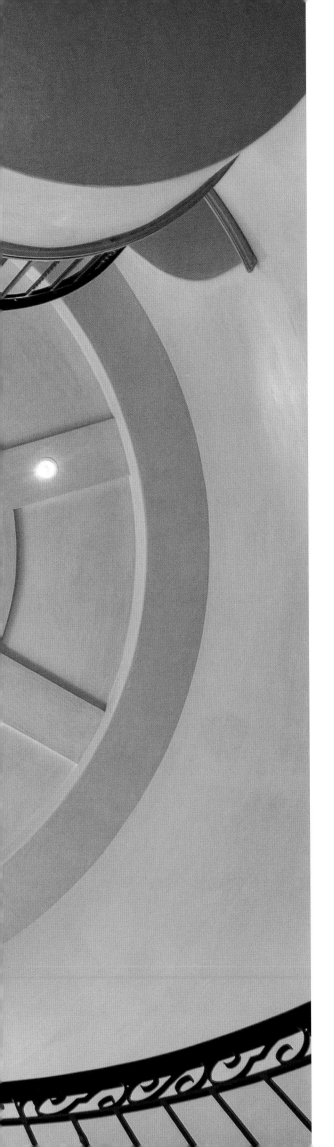

Work OF ART

Designer - Cherry Curlet
Architect - Murphy Mears Architects
Builder - University Towne Building Corporation

EXPRESSING BEAUTY, GRACE AND THE HOMEOWNERS' passion for art, this home's sleek modern style showcases the diverse art collection it houses. To work with both the minimalist architecture and comfortable furnishings, the walls and floors remained as neutral as possible. Without baseboards, plaster covers the entire surface, creating a seamless transition from white wall to limestone floor.

Artwork by Rob Reasoner. Chandelier from "Nastro" Collection, Andromeda.
Light fixtures throughout from Leucos. Limestone floors from Leuders Limestone.

"Unlike the original lath and plaster method, veneer plaster over sheetrock allows the use of regular nails, making it easy to display artwork."

Left: Lithograph above mantel by Edvard Munch. Above: Gold leaf table by Yves Klein. Large couches from Armani/Casa. Artwork, clockwise from far left, by Henri de Toulouse-Latrec, Pierre-Auguste Renoir, Rembrandt van Rijn, Pablo Picasso, Henri de Toulouse-Latrec, Pierre-Auguste Renoir and Henri Matisse.

Left: Round table and chairs from Armani/Casa. Artwork by Dorothy Hood. Right: Lithograph, "The Death Chamber," by Edvard Munch.

Artwork, from left to right, by Man Ray and Kathe Kollwitz.

European MANOR

Designer - Kara Childress

ALTHOUGH THE ARCHITECTURE OF THIS HOME resembles that of an English manor, the interiors reveal the homeowners' European travels. French and Italian influences are evident in the furnishings and accessories. Plaster, crafted with minimal modeling and the softest of sheens, balances the ball gown-like fabrics used for draperies and upholstered pieces.

Demilune table, French gilt mirror and 18th c. French barometer from Tara Shaw. Antique French fauteuil from Joyce Horn Antiques. Satin fabric from Nancy Corzine.

"Painted sheetrock cannot convey the same richness and European flair of a plastered wall. Achieving formality and warmth simultaneously, plaster transforms a newly constructed home into one of past centuries."

Center monastery table from Edward Ferrell. Marble-topped French tea table from Joyce Horn Antiques. Antique pillows from Watkins Culver Antiques. Pair of antique French chairs from Found. Oushak rug from Creative Flooring Resources.

Above: Draperies from G&S Custom Draperies. Fabric from Nancy Corzine. Trim from Décor de Paris at Allan Knight & Associates. Pair of antique French chairs from Tara Shaw. Custom dining chairs from Neal & Co. Upholstery. Fabric from Groves Bros. Fabrics. 18th c. console from Joyce Horn Antiques. Oushak rug from Carol Piper Rugs. Mirror from Empire Antiques. Right: Table from Minton-Spidell Incorporated. Reclaimed barn wood siding from The Woodshop of Texas.

Embracing a more casual feel,

textured plaster evokes a touch of rusticity to balance the
reclaimed barn wood used for the window and cabinetry.

Wine Room Architect - Newberry Campa Architects, LLC

"Gypsum plasters are much more durable than paint or faux finishes. Just like real stone, the pigment is evenly distributed through the product, making dings easy to repair by lightly sanding. The density of plaster prevents it from absorbing oils."

Classic COUNTRY FRENCH

Designer - Terry Harmon
Architect - Hollenbeck Architects, Inc.
Builder - Black Diamond Properties

COUNTRY FRENCH IN FEEL WITH AN ENGAGING MIX of antiques and cozy, upholstered pieces, this home is both casual and inviting. The plaster and special wood finishes add another dimension to the rooms and further emphasize the warmth of the home. The furniture finish of the cabinetry blends with the surrounding antiques.

Lamp, 19th c. French chair and side table from Joyce Horn Antiques.

Gascogne blue limestone island top, Lagos Azul limestone backsplash and perimeter counter from Walker Zanger.

19th c. Louis XIII arm chairs and 19th c. French sofa table from Joyce Horn Antiques. Garden seats from AREA. Linen drapery fabric from Stark Fabric.
Trim from Samuel & Sons. 18th c. French side table from Janet Wiebe Antiques. Lamp and custom shade from Festoni. Floors from Custom Floors Unlimited.

Iron drapery rod from Iron Accents. Embroidered linen drapery fabric from GP & J Baker. Trim from Lee Jofa.

"I love how the neutrality of the plaster in the home's main areas showcases the brick and stone, while the introduction of strong colors in accent pieces complements the reclaimed materials and furnishings in the living and dining areas."

European FARMHOUSE

Designer - Eleanor Cummings
Building Design - Robert Dame Designs
Builder - Memorial Builders Inc.

TO CREATE THE AUTHENTIC FEEL OF AN OLD European farmhouse that has been renovated and updated, reclaimed materials are built in, becoming the grounding factor of the home's design. The age-old flooring, beams, brick and stone become architectural features that truly make this newly constructed home one of yesteryear with plenty of history.

THE SERENE BLUE PLASTER accentuates the beautiful Oushak rug in this living room. By applying a customized glaze to the baseboards and window casings, the trim disappears.

Oushak rug from Carol Piper Rugs. Fireplace mantel, reclaimed stone and brick from Chateau Domingue.

THE
WONDERFUL
COLORS

of the dining room generate
interest by playing off the fabrics
and furnishings. The antique
doors, integrating a bit of the
room's terracotta tone, recall
the hues of an Italian villa the
homeowners had visited.

A GRAY WASH

over the bathroom cabinets maintains and softens their rustic appearance.

"In situations where the railing meets
the wall, the plaster installation needs to
happen first. Make sure that your plasterer
is able to repair since railing installation
can damage the walls."

Sink and door from Chateau Domingue.

"One of my favorite features of plaster is its ability to transform a space and create a coziness otherwise difficult to achieve in rooms with twenty foot ceilings."

Continental EUROPEAN

Designer - Kara Childress
Building Design - Robert Dame Designs
Builder - Parker House Inc.
Architectural Consultant - Sarah West

TO ENHANCE THE EUROPEAN FLAIR OF THE ARCHITECTURE AND accentuate the stone and beam details, plaster on the walls and ceilings of the common areas brings warmth and character to this newly constructed home. Offering more variation to the finish than a smooth plaster, the textured, gypsum plaster that was applied over all the sheetrock surfaces achieves intimacy within the high-ceilinged, spacious rooms. By creating a light and airy backdrop in this open floor plan, the depth of the art and tapestries adds drama to the space, while gentle glazes on the cabinetry match the character of the plaster and provide a lived-in, homey feel.

French settee from Found. Lamps from Maison Maison. Demilunes from Brown. Louis Philippe mirrors from Joyce Horn Antiques. Chandelier from W. Gardner, Ltd. Antique pillows from Becky Vizzard at Watkins Culver Antiques. Oushak rug from Creative Flooring Resources. Antique French painting "Lady by the Well" from Chateau Domingue. Silver crosses from Longoria Collection. Coffee table from Vieux Interiors. Altarstick from Janet Wiebe Antiques transformed into lamp by Lighting Treasures. Floors from AR Floor Designs of Houston.

THIS KITCHEN AND DEN AREA

offers an ideal place to entertain, cook and celebrate traditions. Glazing on the cabinetry brings the cabinets into the room, making them part of the furnishings. Matching the antique mirror, the finish on the sink cabinet customizes this powder bathroom.

Stone range hood from Materials Marketing. Lamp from Aidan Gray. Antique walnut wine tasting table from AREA. Baroque floral fabric on chair and draperies from Scalamandre. Woven shades from Hartmann & Forbes. Custom sofa linen fabric from Rogers & Goffigon. Antler chandelier from Vieux Interiors. Rug from Creative Flooring Resources. Coffee table from Mecox Gardens. Antique stone doe and baluster lamps from 2 Lucy's. Sofa table from Restoration Hardware. Right: Mirror from Joyce Horn Antiques.

THE SMOOTH GYPSUM

plaster on the walls of this light-filled dining room echoes the pale blues of the pair of 18th century French panels. Flowing nicely between the kitchen and dining room, the pale slate blue of the cabinet finish lends a custom feel to this simple bar space while the hardware adds a European touch.

Panels from 2 Lucy's. Painted buffet from Mecox Gardens. Antique Italian chandelier from Twenty Six Twenty Antiques. Oushak rug from Creative Flooring Resources. Custom table and chairs from Neal & Co. Upholstery. Linen velvet fabric from Travers & Co. Antique sconces from Waltkins Culver Antiques. Antique French altarsticks from Joyce Horn Antiques. French gilt mirror from Memorial Antiques & Interiors, MAI. Custom drapery panels throughout the home from G&S Custom Draperies. Fabric from Great Plains. Trim from Samuel & Sons.

GYPSUM PLASTER

MADE PRIMARILY FROM A MIXTURE OF GYPSUM, many of these plasters have some lime and marble dust added. This plaster provides a strong, hard surface that resists abrasions and surface cracking and can easily be repaired by a knowledgeable plasterer. Working best in medium to light colors, gypsum plaster is low Volatile Organic Compounds (VOC). Since the pigments used to tint the product often contain higher VOC elements, insist that low VOC pigments are used if this is a concern. The product can be manipulated to be smooth like porcelain or more distressed by using a skip trowel technique. This plaster works as a sound barrier, insulating factor, and slight fire retardant. It is well-priced and can go over taped and sanded sheetrock or a previously painted wall.

AMERICAN CLAY PLASTER

MADE FROM CLAY, AGGREGATE, MINERAL PIGMENTS and a non-toxic mold inhibitor, this plaster has no VOC and does not fade in color over time. These clay plasters absorb odor as well as humidity in the environment helping to regulate heating and cooling when a substantial portion of the home is plastered. Although easily repaired even by the homeowner, this plaster is softer. American Clay strongly suggests using their own colors to maintain the no VOC properties of the product and can customize pigments for a charge. This plaster, a bit earthier in appearance, can be troweled smooth or with a textured finish. Because this is a two-part plastering system, it is typically more expensive than gypsum-based plasters.

JAPANESE PLASTER

MADE PRIMARILY FROM DIATOMACEOUS EARTH, this plaster has no VOCs and is very durable. Simply use a damp cloth to clean the surface. It has air purifying and sound dampening characteristics. Sand, straw and seaweed can be added to give the plaster texture and interest. While there are many colors to choose from, having Japanese plaster tinted requires a 60 bag minimum. An ideal product for bathrooms, some of the plasters are completely water resistant. Because there are limited quantities in the United States, the shipping or wait time can be substantial.

MADE FROM A FINE LIME PUTTY AND MARBLE DUST, this plaster is readily available. The VOC count fluctuates depending on whether Venetian plaster is made in a synthetic version or all natural. Able to hold rich, intense pigments, this plaster has the sheen of a polished marble slab and more variation than the other plasters discussed. Venetian plaster is a layering plaster, requiring three coats to give that polished marble finish, followed by a coat of wax. Though durable in finish, it is very difficult to repair, even by a knowledgeable installer. Creating a jewel box effect in smaller spaces such as powder rooms or dining rooms, this plaster is a bit strong for allover house applications.

SHEETROCK MUD

SHEETROCK MUD, WHEN APPLIED WITH A TROWEL to create texture, is often labeled as plaster. Although the result is beautiful when done correctly, this method is a faux technique replicating plaster treatments. Once applied for texture, the sheetrock mud is primed, painted and glazed lending more variation and accentuating the texture underneath. This product can also be pigmented like plasters and applied in a layering process to replicate an aged wall that has chipped away to reveal previous paint colors. Rough to the touch, this product can be repaired by a knowledgeable faux artist.

Rug from Matt Camron Rugs & Tapestries. Chandelier and lamp from Alcon Lightcraft Co. Antique French birdbath from Jacques Antiques. Antique French chair, settee, fireplace screen and altarsticks from Joyce Horn Antiques. Buffet from Pettigrew Associates.

SECTION 2
Winning COMBINATIONS

THIS HOME AND THE OTHERS THAT FOLLOW REVEAL A VARIETY OF TECHNIQUES THAT lend each space a custom look, while still maintaining a continuous flow. While some homes call for a single finish throughout, others combine multiple finishes - a mixture of furniture and cabinet finishes, plaster, paint, hand painted designs and murals - to complement an individual design or architectural style.

TO SUCCESSFULLY VARY THE COLORS of this music room and the living room flanking the entry, the same finish on the crown molding maintains continuity between the two rooms. Distressing and aging these mahogany chairs from early marriage revamped them to fit in with the new room's decor.

Above: Artwork over sofa from Frame Tek Art Services. Antique screen and side table from Joyce Horn Antiques.
Rug from Oriental Rug Gallery of Texas. Right: French Trumeau mirror and confit pot from Joyce Horn Antiques.

Transforming the former

garage into a welcoming back entrance, the loose French tree mural adds quaintness to the space while the furniture finish on the cabinetry contributes a polished look. The continuation of the design on the ceiling heightens the room and ties in the colors of the floor. The hand painted French inspired painting on the side of the refrigerator panel ties together the color combinations used in this kitchen/breakfast room.

Right: Plaster medallion and sconces from Joyce Horn Antiques. Floors from Materials Marketing. Above: Granite counters from Canyon Marble & Granite. Concrete counter from Gunnells Concrete Designs, Inc. Tiles from Walker Zanger. Chairs and chandelier from Carl Moore Antiques. Antique French painting and sconces from Joyce Horn Antiques.

It's all about THE COLOR

Designer - Nicole Zarr
Building Design - Colby Design
Builder - University Towne Building Corporation

ADDING A BIT OF PLAYFULNESS, THE COWTAN & TOUT drapery fabric served as inspiration. Coated in gypsum plaster, the walls and ceiling correspond with the colors from the stone floors. Painted green and stenciled in warm brown, the hand-embellished ceiling pulls colors from the draperies to carry out the cohesive color scheme.

Antique console from Maison Maison. Light fixtures from Tara Shaw. Custom artwork by Leslie Sinclair from Segreto Studios.

"To add a little punch, while still allowing the room
to flow with the plastered entrance, we decided to
have fun with the ceiling step-up detail."

THIS FRENCH BLUE

plaster connects the colors used in the rest of the home.

End tables from Joyce Horn Antiques. Fabric from Vervain. Artwork by Rachel Schwind from Segreto Studios. Mantel from Materials Marketing.

FOR A CRISP, CLEAN LOOK

in the kitchen, the lighter
walls blend with the living
room's plaster. A different color
on the island and edging details
on all cabinetry pull out the
fabric tones and add charm.

*Range hood from Materials Marketing. Tile from
Architectural Design Resource, ADR.*

Bench from Liz Spradling Antiques. Lanterns from Brown.

"After pricing fabric to upholster the walls of the back hallway, we decided on a paint treatment instead because of cost and greater durability."

ADDING DESIGNS IN PASSAGEWAYS

creates unique, intimate spaces. Keeping a neutral backdrop but injecting a hint of blue, a cherry blossom motif embellishes the walls of this hallway. The stencil pattern decorates the pass-through between his-and-hers master bathroom.

"This house is a project dear to my heart. Inspiration for most homes begins with a color swatch, but here raising money for an important cause was my driving force."

Pink RIBBON

Entrance Designer - Katie Galliano
Dining Room Designer - Julia Blailock
Family Room and Kitchen Designer - Suzanne Duin
Master Suite Designer - Julie Dodson
Architect - Hollenbeck Architects, Inc.
Builder - Levitt Partnership

THE HOUSTON PINK RIBBON HOUSE provided interior designers with the opportunity to help raise funds to support breast cancer awareness and research at Baylor College of Medicine.

Each designer was awarded a different room or area as her project. To connect their unique styles, a unifying factor was needed to bring depth and substance to the open floor plan.

Creating a warm and established feel, an authentic plaster finish was chosen for the walls and ceilings to add richness and sophistication. Decorative glazed finishes were added to cabinetry, and several walls were fashioned with hand painted designs to make each space distinct.

With the chandelier for inspiration, a painted medallion highlights the vaulted ceiling, and this well-designed entry provides a promise of beautiful rooms to come.

Entrance lantern from Tara Shaw. Rugs from Creative Flooring Resources. Hanging fixture from Brown.

ADDING ARCHITECTURAL WEIGHT,

the distressed faux columns that appear to support the groin vault offset the more textured wall plaster chosen for this room.

Louis XV buffet, dining chairs, chandelier, sconces and Louis Philippe mirror from Carl Moore Antiques. Area rug from Matt Camron Rugs & Tapestries. Host and hostess chairs from Mecox Gardens. Painting from Gremillion & Co. Fine Art, Inc. Accessories from Design House and Krispen.

COMFORTABLE AND BEAUTIFUL

is the feel in this kitchen and family room. Warm walls of creamy plaster, glazed cabinetry and stained beams in a lighter hue than the doors convey an intimate setting for the cozy furnishings in this large space.

Antique Oushak rug from Matt Camron Rugs & Tapestries. Lighting from Visual Comfort & Co. Louis XIV style sofa, chairs, antique pillows and ottoman from Maison Maison. Drop leaf dining table from Carl Moore Antiques. Artwork by Allan Rodewald from Segreto Studios.

By glazing the kitchen cabinets

in the same tones as the walls, the island, inspired by an antique Italian table, takes center stage. Just off the kitchen, the cabinetry in this charming office coordinates with the color of the wall covering. The upper cabinets are darker while the lower cabinets are lighter in tone and embellished with a charcoal hue.

Custom backsplash tile from Architectural Design Resource, ADR. Walnut counter from Canyon Mesquite. Pottery and barstools from Maison Maison.

"When finalizing a color for a
master suite, I always consider
the homeowners' skin tones.
Everyone needs to look beautiful
in their master!"

NEITHER
CONTEMPORARY
NOR TRADITIONAL,
this retreat also combines masculine elements with
a feminine feeling. Although the room is neutral,
stunning hand painted floral trees decorate the
walls. A splash of pink in the painted flowers picks
up the pillows and accessories in the room.

Above: Bed, chair, chaise longue and nightstands from The Joseph Company. Bedding from Plush Home. Starburst and antique bench from Watkins Culver Antiques. Rug from Creative Flooring Resources. Draperies from Heine's Custom Draperies. Lamps from Circa Lighting. Left: Dutch Baroque dropfront desk from Joyce Horn Antiques. Artwork by Kiah Denson from Segreto Studios.

FRENCH *Chateau*

Designers - Margie Slovack and Sarah Herndon
Architect - Sullivan, Henry, Oggero & Associates, Inc.
Builder - Memorial Builders Inc.

FINISHES ARE CRUCIAL WHEN MAKING SELECTIONS for a grand-style home. Accented by crystal pieces and formal furnishings, the open floor plan, marble floors and graceful arches require paint treatments that soften the rooms. A one-color glaze in soft gold tones warms the walls throughout the main areas of the home, allowing the space to be seen in its entirety. Only the high, flat ceilings are left untouched.

Towering archways, under the grand staircase and throughout the home, receive the same finish as the walls, emphasizing the architecture.

A HAND PAINTED FRENCH

design highlights each groin apex and adds elegance. Bronzes and golds applied to the formerly cream-colored lanterns harmonize with the home's décor. Leading into the dramatic two-story, paneled living room, a series of glazes and gilded highlights enhance the elaborate carved details of the room, imparting a rich patina and character.

A SEQUENCE OF GLAZES

in the kitchen enriches the intricate cabinet designs. The kitchen backsplash, mimicking a rug design with tiles, fills the space behind the cooktop and provides a colorful focal point. The plastered range hood carries that focal interest to the ceiling.

Mosaic and tile backsplash from Materials Marketing.

"Carrying the same textured plaster onto the pitched ceilings allows the large spaces to feel cozier while accentuating the beams, brick and flooring."

Relaxed TRADITIONAL

Designer - Jean Ellen Russell
Building Design - Robert Dame Designs
Builder - Steve Burns, Centamark Custom Homes
Accessories and Furnishings - The Accessory Place

TRANSITIONING FROM A ONE-STORY RANCH, the homeowners wanted to make this spacious Mediterranean-influenced home feel more comfortable, casual and traditional to correspond with their personal taste and lifestyle. By interlacing some treasured antiques with newer furnishings, the home exudes an old-world elegance but with all the modern conveniences.

Antique mirror from Jacques Antiques. Shelves over arches from Memorial Antiques & Interiors, MAI.

Island counter from Custom Floors Unlimited.

"Because the crown molding creates a natural stopping point, painting the ceiling to match the plaster tricks the eye and offers budget savings."

PULLING OUT COLORS

and design elements from the room, the decorative painting that embellishes the range hood emulates the scroll designs both in the light fixture and on the glass door of the butler's pantry.

BY APPLYING INDIVIDUAL
finishes to the custom-built cabinetry, the
cabinets become part of the home's furnishings,
serving more than just a utilitarian function.
Stenciled walls in similar tones to the plaster
increase the formality of the dining room and
make for an easy transition to other rooms.

"The soothing, temperate color palette we used in this room gives this elegantly styled bedroom the whisper of a retreat...just the respite these homeowners needed!"

AN ELEGANT, SUBTLE

and cost-effective alternative, a one-color wash on the walls warms the space. For vaulted ceilings, the principle of using the same finish on both ceiling and wall still applies.

"Ornamental accents are first drawn on paper to form the pattern. Just as with sewing, a round patterning tool is rolled over the design, poking little holes in the drawing. The pattern is then taped to the wall, and charcoal is applied over the design, leaving a guide through the holes that can subsequently be painted. This method ensures uniformity when using a repetitive embellishment."

Magical MEDITERRANEAN

Designer - Sheila Lyon
Builder - Iraj Taghi Custom Homes

LEAVING BEHIND THE STYLE OF THEIR PREVIOUS, TRADITIONAL GEORGIAN home, the homeowners embraced the Mediterranean architecture dictated by their new household. Prior to purchase, walls of the main area were already completed, but the individual spaces still needed some artful touches. A hand painted design now elegantly appoints the archways, tying in the soft gold hues used throughout the home.

THE NEWLY PLASTERED dining room repeats the gold accents present throughout the home, while the metallic faux finish of the ceiling dome showcases the handcrafted, rock crystal chandelier. The powder room is turned into a dazzling jewel box with the use of Venetian plaster, dramatic in appearance and slick to the touch. The stone rope design, hand painted on the groin vault, adds an embellishment that complements the stone and completes the look.

Right: Floors from Walker Zanger.

"In most cases, the surfaces of the home - counters, tiles, flooring and fabrics - should be chosen before finish colors are finalized."

INSPIRED BY THE TURKISH THROW, single-color soft ragging covers the walls and ceilings. When the treatment spills onto the ceiling, it's important to have the vents painted as well. The color of the textured plaster is culled from the master sitting area.

Mirror from Joyce Horn Antiques. Night stand from Marge Carson. Drapery fabric from B. Berger Fabrics.

Bench from Liz Spradling Antiques. Oushak rug from Stark Fabric. Consoles from Brian Stringer Antiques. Coffee table from Minton-Spidell Incorporated.

"The plaster takes the room to a level that sheetrock alone cannot, giving the space depth and sophistication. The plastered walls showcase the custom-made fireplace and create the effect that the antique plaques flanking the fireplace are embedded in thick walls."

Comfortable LUXURY

Designer - Julia Blailock
Building Design - Robert Dame Designs
Builder - Memorial Builders Inc.

ALTHOUGH THIS HOME HAS A MEDITERRANEAN architectural style, the design leans more toward continental European, mixing antiques with interesting textures and contemporary art with more traditional pieces. Just as the furnishings are mixed, the home also merges a variety of decorative treatments, including plasters, faux and hand painted finishes.

The Oushak rug, with its pale blues, creams and touches of gold, tells the color story of the entire house. While maintaining a warm, neutral palette, the homeowners' love of blue is gracefully woven into various accents throughout.

THE SOFT GRAY-BLUE

plaster in this room
plays off the needlepoint
rug. With the coved
walls flowing into the
ceiling, the plaster
envelops the room and
creates a wonderful,
intimate space.

*Mirror from Minton-Spidell
Incorporated. Sconces from
Panache Lighting. Prints from
AREA. Chandelier from
Currey & Company.*

TO REPLICATE EUROPEAN STYLE, the ceiling of this living area is stenciled, hand-embellished and tea-stained. Drawing the eye upward, this design enhances the beams and light fixture. With hints of blue in the furnishings, the splash of red on the ceiling of the study evokes drama and masculinity, tying in the draperies. A Ralph Lauren stencil design inside the coffers is painted in brown and covered with a tea stain, tempering the red background color and complementing the paneling and floors.

Artwork by Linda Dautreil. Light fixture from Lighting, Inc. Rug from Pride of Persia Rug Co.

Light fixture from Currey & Company. Rug from Stark Fabric. Shade from Conrad Shades. Drapery fabric from Robert Allen. Chair fabric from Donghia.

THE MASTER BATH
has a terrific rotunda with access to
the separate tub area and his-and-her
spaces. Glazing walls in a soft color
wash brings warmth to the space
without the need for a lot of pattern.

"I love that the framing of the floating egg prints allows
you to see the beautiful plaster walls underneath so that
the wall becomes part of the art itself."

Ranch RENOVATION

Designer - Talbot Cooley
Building Design - Colby Design

DIFFERING CEILING HEIGHTS THROUGHOUT THE HOUSE PRESENTED A
challenge in making adjacent areas of the home flow. A contiguous feel from plastering
walls and ceilings in these areas causes the height discrepancies to seem intentional.
Prior to renovation, the space off the entry was grand yet seemed cold. The large
sheetrock ceiling, offset by the brick, had noticeable seams and imperfections that
really stood out, especially at night. Plaster truly evolved the space. All the issues
disappeared and the ceiling became just another part of the room.

Egg prints from Frame Tek Art Services. Rug from Pride of Persia Rug Co.
Lamps from Aidan Gray. Light fixture from Antiques at Dunlavy.

"If you can't find antique doors that work,
buy new ones and finish them to your liking.
Purchasing new doors and giving them
an old patina is often less expensive than
investing in refurbished ones."

THE KITCHEN, OPEN TO THE DEN, is the household's hub. Cabinet glazes and antique hexagonal tiles, reclaimed from a French convent, give this newly built kitchen an old world European ambiance. By distressing the look and applying gesso under the glazes, the French blue pantry doors assume the appearance of salvaged antique treasures. The glazed built-ins create continuity between the kitchen and den.

Tile backsplash from Chateau Domingue. Light fixtures from Joyce Horn Antiques.

SIMPLE AND REFINED, the glazed walls and stenciled ceiling draw the eye up and add softness.

Floors and counters from Walker Zanger. Chandelier and sconces from Marburger Farm Antique Show.

One of three sets, these doors adorn the walls of the existing long, narrow hallway. Instead of doing major construction, the French design painted on the doors visually opens the space, making the corridor feel more spacious.

Drapery fabric from George Cameron Nash. Sofa fabric from Pindler & Pindler. Chair fabric from Robert Allen.

NEW ORLEANS *Charm*

VARIATIONS OF WARM TAUPE COMPRISE the color palette of this New Orleans style home. Plastering the walls and ceilings adds subtle drama to the entryway, forming a soft, welcoming backdrop for the home's architecture, artwork and furnishings. The glazed woodwork highlights the substantial, custom milled moldings and serves as a connecting factor that transitions the wall color and texture changes throughout the home.

Designer - John Kidd
Building Design - Colby Design
Builder - R. D. Allen Inc.

19th c. Sultanabad rug from Goravanchi Co. Persian Rugs. Runner from Stark Fabric. 17th c. Flemish tapestry from Carol Piper Rugs.

PULLING THE BLUES from the draperies, a hand-drawn and painted pattern creates a wallpaper feel in the dining room, while the fabric walls in the living room offer texture. To bring character and depth to the study, a series of glaze washes in the same taupe as the rest of the home makes the space warm without necessitating a dark stained look.

Above: Baccarat chandelier from Keil's Antiques. Drapery fabric from George Cameron Nash. Above right: "Summer Hill" sofa from Hamilton Furniture and Textiles. Sofa fabric from Marvic Textiles. Paper-backed linen wall covering from Walter Lee Culp & Assoc. Drapery fabric from Koplavitch & Zimmer. Tabriz rug from Goravanchi Co. Persian Rugs.

COUNTRYSIDE *Manor*

Designer - Cindy Witmer
Architectural Consultant - Sarah West
Building Design - Robert Dame Designs
Builder - Parker House Inc.

TO COMPLEMENT THE ANTIQUE surfaces in this home, finishes created patina and aged the newly constructed, built-in elements. Paint treatments on beams, focal point doors and cabinetry convey a great deal of character, melding in the new with the authentic reclaimed oak flooring, stone fireplaces and antique doors. A neutral paint palette on walls and ceilings permits the eye to focus on and appreciate the wonderful architectural elements of the home.

Antique French stone mantel and European sconces from Chateau Domingue. Artwork by Leslie Sinclair from Segreto Studios. Daybed and French chairs from Marburger Farm Antique Show. Chandelier from Tara Shaw. Oushak rug from Creative Flooring Resources. Stone table from Memorial Antiques & Interiors, MAI. Furniture from Hien Lam Upholstery. Fabric from Pindler & Pindler. Floors from AR Floor Designs of Houston.

reveals how a finish transformed these formerly unimpressive, new doors into an enchanting, "old" passageway. They look and feel distinctive, yet retain the durability of mahogany wood.

REMINISCENT of centuries-old walls in aged European manors, this stencil, applied over a textured sheetrock mud, suggests a worn look by allowing unevenness in its application.

Left: Table from Restoration Hardware. Chandelier from Liz Spradling Antiques. Zinc sideboard from AREA. Rugs from Creative Flooring Resources. Drapery throughout by Linda Falk. Right: Antique French bathroom door from Joyce Horn Antiques. Reclaimed marble sink from Chateau Domingue. Sconces from Marburger Farm Antique Show.

JUST AS OLD AND NEW FINISHES MIX TOGETHER,

old and new tiles intermingle in the kitchen, conveying warmth while
preserving the space's prevalent clean lines.

Left: Artwork by Rachel Schwind from Segreto Studios. Chandelier from Vieux Interiors. Rug from Creative Flooring Resources. Chair fabric from Rogers & Goffigon. Sconces from Memorial Antiques & Interiors, MAI. Fireplace screen from Marburger Farm Antique Show. Above: Kitchen tiles from Chateau Domingue and Materials Marketing. Light fixtures from Liz Spradling Antiques.

Through a Hand-Distressed

treatment and stains in alternating combinations of light and dark, these solid Douglas fir beams have the look of age-old reclaimed wood without the expense.

Upholstery by Hien Lam Upholstery. Silk and bamboo velvet fabric on headboard from Scalamandre. Bedding from Longoria Collection. Settee from Memorial Antiques & Interiors, MAI. Lamps from Aidan Gray. Drapery fabric from Peter Fasano. Custom rug from Creative Flooring Resources.

Ranch-style CHATEAU

Designer - Talbot Cooley

Building Design - Colby Design & Brandon Breaux

Builder - Darryl Dieciedue

THIS HOME, BUILT TO NOT ONLY TO ENTERTAIN BUT also to provide a comfortable, welcoming environment for the homeowners' growing extended family, incorporates an open floor plan and large spaces with room for everyone to gather. With high vaulted ceilings, gypsum plaster conveys a more intimate setting. Quality finishes soften the beautiful custom cabinetry throughout, making it part of the home's furnishings. Detailed touches adorn selected walls and ceilings, adding uniqueness to individual spaces.

Above: Diptych artwork by Leslie Sinclair from Segreto Studios. Right: Antique heart pine floors from Custom Floors Unlimited. Artwork over mantel from Chateau Domingue. Fireplace from Alamo Stone Company. Chocolate mohair on sofa from Rose Tarlow Melrose House. Club chair fabric from Kravet. Lamps from Boxwood Interiors.

Custom light fixture over island from Brown. Island countertop from Chateau Domingue. Accessories from Joyce Horn Antiques.

TO BALANCE

the industrial components
of the concrete counters and
the elegance of the mirrors
and sconces, a tone-on-tone
tree mural and aged cabinet
finish imbue the space
with a subtle grace.

Left: Concrete counters from
Gunnells Concrete Designs Inc.
Light fixtures from Elegant
Additions. Right: Buffet from
Joyce Horn Antiques. Sconces from
Currey & Company.

"Bringing artful touches to the walls and ceilings of this large 21st century
construction transforms its newness into the richness of a home with history."

COVERED IN ARENA DESIGN WALLPAPER,
the dining room still needed some finishing touches to lend a warmer, more custom look. A hand
painted medallion on the ceiling enhances both the Murano glass chandelier and the wonderful
pattern on the walls. New finishes enable these homeowners to use existing furnishings such as
the originally gold-leafed mirror that was re-painted in metallic to complement the wallpaper.

THE MASTER BEDROOM presents a spa retreat. Continuing the plaster into the master bathroom with areas for him and her harmonizes the separate rooms into one space. The bath evolves into a furnished room through the use of special paint touches on the cabinetry, the doors leading to the coffee bar and the shades on the sconces. Because the scale of the chosen wallpaper was too wide to fit the door insets, a painted mural demonstrates a better option, wrapping around the doors for a finished look.

Left: Herbiers from Frame Tek Art Services. Chandelier from Canopy Designs Ltd. Lamps from Restoration Hardware. "Bella" bedding from Kuhl-Linscomb. Right: Marble and tile from Walker Zanger. Sinks and light fixtures from Elegant Additions.

"With soothing tones of plaster
on the walls and ceilings that
blend with the soft color
palette of the furnishings, this
is truly a place to relax."

"These homeowners love to entertain and visit with family and friends. Their gatherings often necessitate moving upholstered pieces from room to room, so we focused on picking finishes and colors that would accommodate changes to the furnished layout of the home."

Timeless, ELEGANT & LIVABLE

Designer - Anne Lydick

THE ENTRY HALL SETS THE COLOR PALETTE FOR the rest of this traditional home, giving guests a warm welcome.

Each space is designed to flow gracefully into the next while maintaining an individuality of its own. The gypsum plastered, smooth walls and ceilings in the entrance, formal living and hallways create a wonderful backdrop for the home's collection of antiques.

An assortment of finishes throughout this gracious home embellishes its classic, traditional look.

Louis XV commode from Carl Moore Antiques. Antique Persian Senneh rug from Matt Camron Rugs & Tapestries. William and Mary cabinet from Britannia Antiques.

ONE OF THE COZIEST

rooms in the house is this wood-paneled library. The painted, faux wood beams and tiles on the ceiling add character to the room without necessitating major construction.

Rug from Matt Camron Rugs & Tapestries. Fabrics from Brunschwig & Fils. Artwork by Henri Schouten.

"The breakfast room, kitchen, den and back powder walls are adorned with a rich terracotta Venetian plaster. Venetian plasters can hold deep rich pigments and although durable, can be difficult to repair if damaged."

Above: 18th c. Louis XV French walnut Vaissilier a Horlage from Carl Moore Antiques. Italian chandeliers and sconces from Joyce Horn Antiques. Artwork by Donna Phipps Stout from Valley House Gallery. Rug from Emmet Perry & Co. Drapery fabric from Bailey & Griffin. Left: 19th c. Normandy bonnetiere built into the wall, Provencal buffet, sconces and mirror from Joyce Horn Antiques. Sink and faucets from Westheimer Plumbing & Hardware. Rug from Matt Camron Rugs & Tapestries. Right: Mirror from Carl Moore Antiques. Sink and faucets from Westheimer Plumbing & Hardware.

INSPIRED BY A FRESCO PAINTED IN 1500

at Torre di Bellosguardo, a former hunting lodge outside of Florence, this dramatic rendition is framed by trompe-l'oeil stone columns and archways. The scene incorporates the built-in sink basin to avoid interruptions in the mural.

THIS QUIET SUITE enveloped by smooth gypsum plaster is a perfect hideaway for guests. To avoid adding additional elements to the adjoining bath, the faux finished molding mimics the stone while the cabinet over the toilet mirrors the antique sink basin.

Above: Fabrics from Duralee Fabrics and Brunschwig & Fils. Painted chest and mirror from Joyce Horn Antiques. Coverlets from Plush Home. Pillows from Boxwood Interiors. Lamps from Heather Bowen Antiques. Right: Bathroom sink cabinet and mirror from Joyce Horn Antiques. Sink and faucets from Westheimer Plumbing & Hardware. Stone from Materials Marketing. Engravings from Allart Framing & Gallery.

$\mathcal{E}$nglish PENTHOUSE

Designer - Marjorie Carter
Builder - Builders West, Inc.

THIS ENGLISH PENTHOUSE RIGHT IN THE HEART OF Houston, acts as a gathering place for family and friends and showcases the owners' wonderful collection of antiques. Incorporating reclaimed elements found in London transformed the empty shell into this English country home. Four hundred year-old English oak flooring, antique fireplace surrounds, a hand-hammered balustrade and centuries-old doors instill the home with a sense of history.

Rather than

being built with sheetrock, the walls of
the formal areas are paneled and then
glazed in subtle variations of similar
tones. This layering adds soft shadows
to the paneling, giving them an elegance
and refinement that delicately blends
with the homeowners'
collected treasures.

Calcutta-Oro Italian marble entry floors. 18th c. English lacquered
chest from Jas Gundry Antiques. 18th c. English salt glazed stoneware
collection, 1720-1780.

INSPIRED BY THE COLORS

in the family room, the red cabinets are coated with a brown stain to tie in with the beams and paneling in the adjacent room.

Turkish Oushak rug from Togar Rugs. Floors from Schenck & Company. 19th c. Russian chandelier from Fireside Antiques. 18th c. English painting "Lady with a Rose." 19th c. Chinese export porcelain collection.

"The combination of rich creams and soft blues on the antiqued paneling lends a tasteful backdrop to the room's prominent art and furnishings."

19th c. English mahogany dining table and 18th c. set of chairs from Jas Gundry Antiques. English painting "Haying Wheat," 1869, by John Linnell.

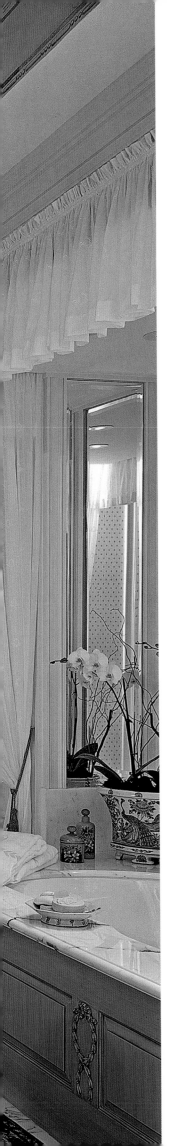

"This master bath turned out as elegant and
refined as the lovely lady who lives there."

TO SYMBOLIZE THE HOMEOWNER'S RECOLLECTION
of her grandmother's sweet pea covered garden, hand painted carvings with decorative
floral and avian corners incorporate both the beloved memories and the architecture
of the antique doors leading to the dressing room. The glazed cabinets also
exhibit the same finish as the 18th century French doors.

19th c. French chair from Brunschwig & Fils. Antique Kayseri silk rug from Togar Rugs. Hand-colored English lithographs of birds, 1802.

LOUIS XV *Revisited*

Antiques and Furnishings
- Joyce Horn Antiques

EVOKING THE SAME style but in a muted palette, this residence suggests the layered and faded appearance of the vivid colors popular in 18th century French homes. Pigmented sheetrock mud in this French blue entrance fades into the nearby creams used in the rest of the home.

By leaving small, irregular gaps when applying two shades of custom-tinted blue gray over cream and terracotta hues, the surfaces give the effect that layers of centuries-old walls have been chipped away, exposing the paint of the past.

This hallway leading to the master suite

contains wonderful treasures from France. By applying the pattern on the ceiling in a watercolor fashion, the paint treatment suggests the same time period as the surrounding antiques.

TO ADD A SENSE OF ARCHITECTURE

to the staircase area, the ceiling color is wrapped onto the walls, and a thin line divides the two tones. This effect, popular in Europe, lifts the lines of the room and adds interest. An ensemble of paint finishes and antiquities in the powder bathroom establish a unified feel modeled after the mosaics and frescoes of Pompeii.

THE ANTIQUE RUG INSPIRED this bedroom's color choices. Applying a panel design with insets of a floral pattern creates a soft effect featuring the antique French wainscoting. A barely-there raw umber stain over the soft blue coved ceiling complements the tones in the rug and artwork. Seeking harmony between the bedroom and nearby sitting room, a faded stripe individualizes the two spaces while the uniform ceiling treatment lends consistency between the rooms. Drawing color cues from existing furnishings, various applications in color treatment add interest.

"Blues intensify in color when applied, so choose a shade with more green or gray than you want it to appear when finished."

CHANGING THE BACKGROUND COLOR OF THIS COVE

creates the illusion that the antique columns are integral parts of the design. Evoking a celestial sky, friezes that decorate these ceilings enhance its architecturally interesting details. 18th century boiserie paneling adorns the walls in the dining room with crown bases and moldings finished to match. The hand painted flowers under the wainscoting complement the tapestry draperies.

*Floors from R.W. Taylor, Inc. Mirror and antique
candlesticks from Joyce Horn Antiques. Chandelier
from Chateau Domingue. Rock crystal lamp and marble
mosaic table from Christie's. Refectory table and
standing candlesticks from Bonhams & Butterfields.
Velvet on chairs from Brunschwig & Fils.*

It feels like HOME

Designer - Sara Howell
Architect - J. Marshall Porterfield, Jr.

THE HOMEOWNERS REVISIT THEIR CHILDHOOD WITH THIS HOME'S DESIGN, inspired by their grandparents' Michigan retreat. Giving the home a warmth that reflects their fond memories, gypsum plastered walls offer an inviting backdrop that flows though the wide traverse hallways connecting the main entertaining areas. Instead of simply occupying a flat plane, the subtlety of this plaster finish defies the viewer to describe what creates that depth, lending a comfortable ambiance to the space.

CARRYING THROUGH THE SAME

plaster used in other parts of the home, the walls of the powder bathroom have a soft metallic stenciled on top. The dining room ceiling, inspired by a villa in Florence, evokes centuries-old elegance and history. Different ceiling finishes in the dining room make this space unique while the wall treatment remains constant throughout the house.

Left: Sink from Christie's. Sconces from Inessa Stewart Antiques. Above: Chandelier from Joyce Horn Antiques. Game table and tapestry chair from Bonhams & Butterfields. Paisley fabric on settee from Etro. Italian jacquard bedding from Signoria Firenze.

Coffee table from Gregorious Pineo at Walter Lee Culp & Assoc. Sofa from Rose Tarlow Melrose House at George Cameron Nash. 19th c. Louis XVI bergeres from The Gray Door. Fabric from Christian Fischbacher. Lamps from Mecox Gardens. Artwork from Gremillion & Co. Fine Art, Inc.

CLASSIC, BEAUTIFUL
&
Welcoming

Designer - John Kidd
Building Design - Colby Design
Builder - Abercrombie Builders Inc.

GIVING THIS NEW CONSTRUCTION THE IMPRESSION OF AN established historical home, gypsum plaster on the walls and ceilings lends a warm and cozy feel. Plaster surfaces instantly relay quality, balancing the fine art and furnishings of this well-dressed interior. To add a bit more depth to the combined hues of gray and gold used in the plasters, waxing the walls brings a richness and porcelain-like refinement to the surfaces.

Antique Oriental Heriz rug from Stark Fabric. Drapery fabric from Ardecora Fabric. Sheers fabric from Rogers & Goffigon. Artwork from Jack Meier Gallery.

"Enhancing the allure of this graceful dining room, the waxed plaster ceiling complements the wonderful motif in the wall covering."

THE RED WALLCOVERING IS BOLD AND DRAMATIC,

so the cabinets needed to be just as lavish and spectacular. To transform this cabinetry into an extraordinary furniture piece, a hand painted, Chinoiserie design on the fronts brings in golds from the fixtures, charcoals from the marble and hints of red from the walls.

Left above: 19th c. Empire dining table from Charlotte Nail Antiques. Chairs from Dessin Fournir Companies. Fabric from Zoffany and Marvic Textiles. Sconces from House of Glass. Late George II hand-carved, gold-leafed mirror from Jas Gundry Antiques. Wall covering from Arena Design. 19th c. Italian chandeliers from Found. Draperies from Rogers & Goffigan. 18th c. Louis XV French enfilade from Kirby Antiques. Above: Wall covering from Arena Design. Empire bronze sconces from House of Glass. Faucet from Sherle Wagner. Late 19th c. Parisian gilt parclose mirror from Joyce Horn Antiques.

The heart of the home is THE KITCHEN

THE KITCHEN'S ROLE HAS EVOLVED OVER THE LAST twenty years. Rather than a separate room to be closed off while entertaining, the kitchen is now the heart of the home. Often open to an adjoining den area, this room has transitioned into the space where family and friends gather and spend time talking to the cook.

In order to integrate kitchens into open designs, cabinetry has evolved as well. Quality finishes turn ordinary built-ins that are typically sprayed one color into unique cupboards that appear to be purchased and incorporated into the design, transforming the kitchen from a simple work area into a delightful space for living and entertaining.

Designer - Kara Childress
Architect - Newberry Campa Architects, LLC
Builder - Windham Builders

19th c. concrete tile backsplash from Chateau Domingue. Reclaimed terracotta floors from Walker Zanger. 18th c. French market counter from Tara Shaw. Chandelier and light fixtures from Annette Schatte Antiques customized by Lighting Treasures.

"Sealing all our cabinet finishes
maintains their beauty over time,
giving them a durability factor that
paint alone cannot achieve."

Designer - Tami Owen
Building Design - Robert Dame Designs
Builder - Stonehenge Classic Homes, Inc.

Reclaimed wood counter from Custom Floors Unlimited.
Light fixtures from Boxwood Interiors. Limestone counter
and tile backsplash from Walker Zanger.

"Rather than changing glazing techniques on the cabinetry in this butler's kitchen area, the cabinet style was altered to give uniqueness and a furniture feel, while keeping the color pallet the same."

Range hood and tile from Architectural Design Resource, ADR.

Designer - Julie Dodson
Builder - Epic Custom Homes

Designer - Pamela Culpepper
Builder - David Levy

"Building glass-front cabinets over the windows fills the room with an open
and airy feel while providing more storage. The vast array of finishes, cabinet
styles and hardware contributes to this thoughtfully designed kitchen."

*Left: Range hood and tile from Architectural Design Resource, ADR. Right: Hardwood floors from Custom Floors Unlimited. Terracotta etched tile backsplash
from Architectural Design Resource, ADR. Granite from Walker Zanger installed by Olympus Marble & Granite. Hardware from Hollywood Builders Hardware.
Sconces from ID Collection. Counter stools from Ellouise Abbott.*

Designer - Donna Minyard
Architect - Charles W. Ligon AIA Architects
Builder - University Towne Building Corporation

"The cabinets painted the same color as the crown molding take on an entirely
different look when glazes are applied to convey the look of furniture."

Designer - Julie Dodson
Builder - Elron Construction Inc

"Built with a rough-cut wood and finished differently than the
other cabinets, these custom pantry doors create character and
interest in this eclectic kitchen."

Handmade pantry doors from Houston Stair Company. Lighting from Heights Lights & Things. Hardware from Morrison Supply Company. Barstools from Muniz Plastics and The Joseph Company. Table from The Joseph Company. Flooring from International Granite & Marble Corp., IGM.

STAINED WOOD AND GLAZED FINISHES

play off each other to bring intrigue to the room. Gypsum plaster on the range hood and antique concrete tiles from a chateau in France give the kitchen a pedigree.

Designer - Maria Tracy
Builder - Crawford Renovations

Bell jar lighting from Lighting, Inc.

255

Designer - Nancy Sharp

Building Design - Colby Design

Builder - Abercrombie Builders Inc.

Above: Granite and tile from Walker Zanger. Right: Chandelier from Joyce Horn
Antiques. Backsplash and floor from Master Tile. Counters from Olympus & Granite.

Renovator - David Levy

"Textured plastered walls combine with glazed cabinetry to conjure the friendly feel of these two kitchens. The center island has a faux wood treatment called faux bois, a painted finish that replicates the look of stained wood."

"Adding interest to this kitchen's plastered range hood, a tone-on-tone design complements the tile backsplash and glazed cabinetry. To establish the built-in buffet as a separate piece in the room, a darker and richer tone than the softened hue of the rest of the kitchen graces the piece."

Designer - Lisa McCollam
Building Design - Colby Design
Builder - Abercrombie Builders Inc.

Lighting from Julie Neill Designs. Tile backsplash and floor from Materials Marketing.
Bar stools from Boxwood Interiors. Hardware from Hollywood Builders Hardware.

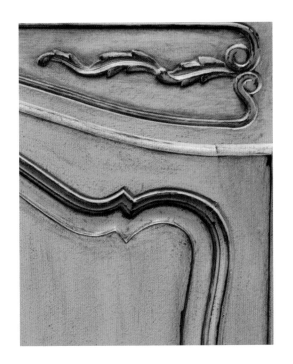
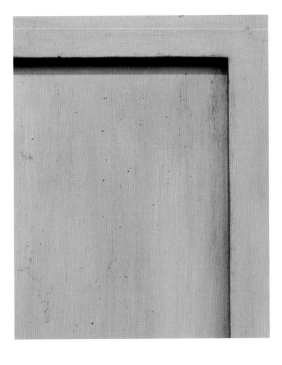

Designer - Tami Owen

"Bathrooms are great spaces to be imaginative with - you can invent a room that is distinctively your own."

Designer - Rachael Miclette

Beautiful BATHS

BECAUSE THERE ARE LIMITED FABRICS AND FURNISHINGS, wall and cabinet finishes are typically the most prevalent factor in bathrooms, dictating their style and mood. Complementing tiles, sinks and hardware, these finishes take a space from ordinary to exceptional.

Dramatic while still aged in feel, to the left, a hand-drawn pattern in iridescent, gold metallic over plaster conveys an elegant, traditional style. Complementing the architecturally interesting ceiling, above, a painted design over plaster dresses up the room and balances the antique cabinets and fixtures.

Left: Mirror and sconces from Brown.
Above: Chandelier from Longoria Collection.

AN UNDERSTATED, SOPHISTICATED AMBIANCE

is cultivated in this master bathroom spa retreat by tying in the tile floor mosaic
with the soft blue grays of the cabinet finish.

Designer - Lisa Dalton

TO HIGHLIGHT THE SINK,

mirror and sconces, the soft shade of the chosen textured plaster lends
sophistication without detracting from the room's focal pieces.

Sink from Chateau Domingue.
Mirror and sconces from Antiques at Dunlavy.

Designer - Cathy Chapman

TERRACOTTA HUES and rich, golden

metallic stenciled in a baroque damask pattern transform
this powder room into one full of glamour. The ceilings are
encrusted with gold leaf and aged with an umber glaze.

Above: Fixtures, sconces and sink from Lighting, Inc. Antique French mirror from Joyce Horn
Antiques. Adjacent page right, above: Tile floor from Walker Zanger.

Designer - Sheila Lyon

A TINTED ARTIST'S GESSO,

troweled through a stencil over a silver metallic paint and then tea stained, gives the appearance of dimensional wallpaper while offering the ability to wrap around corners and arched openings.

INSPIRED BY PAINTINGS

of Old Masters, the mural-adorned cabinet becomes the room's focal element, while the walls have a gentle strié paint finish complementing the cabinet.

A
ONE COLOR
WASH

applied softly gives a faux
plaster look. By using the
same finish for walls and
ceiling, the statue, tiles
and lighting remain the
focus. The cabinets were
embellished to accent
their furniture lines.

*Floor tile and mosaics
from Architectural Design
Resource, ADR. Sconces
from House of Glass. Marble
installed by Olympus Marble
& Granite. Pair of mirrors
from Longoria Collection.
Antique zinc garden statue
from Finnegan Gallery.*

Designer - Donna Minyard
Architect - Charles W. Ligon AIA Architects
Builder - University Towne Building Corporation

Designer - Betty Richter Arnold

THE SILVERY BLUE PLASTERED WALLS ARE LAYERED WITH WAX

to give this bathroom porcelain depth. This treatment provides a beautiful backdrop, highlighting the antique French remnant that serves as a vanity and the mother of pearl wall covering accents on the ceiling and the back of the cabinets.

Antique Venetian mirror from House of Glass. Sconces from George Cameron Nash. Mother of pearl tiles from Stark Fabric. Custom sink from Architectural Design Resource, ADR.

Designer - Anne Lydick

MASTER BATHS ARE
ideal for murals making the space
feel larger because their reflections in
mirrors create the effect that they are
painted completely
around the room.

HAND PAINTED VINES

pull colors from the marble and fabrics
in the adjoining bedroom to fashion a
whimsical yet polished look.

Designer - Sandy Lucas

Designer - Teena Caldwell

Adding a special touch....
FAUX FINISHING

FAUX FINISHING, A TERM THAT DERIVES FROM THE FRENCH WORD "FAUX," meaning "false," describes a wide range of decorative painting techniques. These techniques originated as a way to replicate expensive materials such as marble and wood with paint. The label has subsequently come to encompass many more decorative finishes.

The beginning of the Renaissance in 14th century Europe brought a resurgence of faux painting. Italian painters started using fresco techniques to decorate churches and palaces. This was the golden age for painting, and the prominence of the faux finish trade followed. Many new techniques were developed and existing ones refined, requiring the skills of an observant viewer to discern the real finishes from the faux. Faux wood and faux marble were created and used in the construction of grand cathedrals to keep down the construction costs. Faux finishing today remains an effective way to achieve the desired look and feel at a lower cost than real materials.

Designer - Rita Kissner

TO ACHIEVE A LOOK THAT BALANCES the softness of the drapes with the strength of the desired color, a two-color faux gives the room more dimension than a single paint provides. The first, stronger color brings depth and variation, and the second glaze softens the walls.

REMINISCENT OF

of castles and luxury hotels, yet still
conveying a sense of comfort, the faux finish
warms up the space in an elegant manner.
This family room has a one-color rub
wrapped onto the ceiling to
suggest intimacy.

Designer - Cathy Chapman

Designer - Nancy Sharp

ACCOMPLISHING A

a "been there" feel in a newly constructed
home, a one-color ragging technique
establishes character and warmth. Painting
the ceiling in the same base coat color as
the walls offers a lighter look while
remaining in the same
color palette.

The fifth wall: CEILINGS

ALTHOUGH CEILINGS ENCASE MOST OF A ROOM'S AREA, THIS FIFTH wall is too frequently forgotten. In previous centuries, the ceiling was the most decorated surface in a room. Carved beams, exquisite plaster moldings, elaborate mural work and beautiful color combinations were used to set the tone and personalize the space. While homeowners, inhibited by false myths, have neglected this surface in recent years, the latest trend in ceiling finishes is a return to the centuries-old techniques of hand painted medallions, gold and silver leafing and plaster treatments.

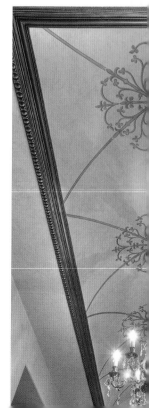

Designer - Teena Caldwell

The art of the
MURAL

MURAL PAINTING IS ONE OF THE OLDEST FORMS of artistic expression. The word "mural," originating from the Latin word "murus" or "wall," refers to any form of visual expression created on a wall. In France, the caves at Lascaux enclose wall paintings dating from 15,000 B.C. One of history's most famous murals, Leonardo da Vinci's *The Last Supper*, 1495 to 1498, was created for the convent refectory of Milan's Santa Maria delle Grazie. During the Baroque period of the 17th century, frescoes on walls gave way to painting on panels, and dramatic wall decorations filled the palaces and villas of northern Europe.

The use of murals in interior design has experienced a revival, attributed in part to diminishing individual living space. Faux architectural features and beautiful views have the effect of expanding walls or ceilings. Murals work wonders to individualize a space and divert the eye from less desirable features, highlighting the room as a whole. Doors often consume the most real estate in the room but become a less prominent component when painted.

Curved staircases, domes, niches and any other areas where it's difficult to hang art are perfect places to decorate with murals. Just like fine art, fine murals have stood the test of time throughout history.

Leave it to the imagination....
STENCILING, STRIPES & DECORATIVE DESIGNS

Designer - Ellie Bale

APPLYING AN ALLOVER PATTERN ON WALLS GIVES A wallpaper feel but offers greater flexibility and practicality. Stenciled and decorative designs achieved with paint eliminate concerns common with wallpapered rooms such as seams pulling up or mold growing behind the surface. One-of-a-kind patterns can be customized with colors and backgrounds to work with any fabric or tile surface, and when it's time for a different look, a single coat of paint can change the finish. Wallpaper, on the other hand, requires paper removal and prepped walls before applying a different treatment. Therefore, paint techniques tend to be less expensive when installation cost is considered.

Historically, some of the first stencils were cut from leaves. Natives of the Fiji Islands used bamboo and banana leaves to make stencils and then pushed vegetable dyes through the cuts onto their bark cloth. Later, in the 17th century, the French began producing wallpaper in the form of stenciled segments called dominoes. These wallpaper dominoes were much cheaper than the expensive cloth that had previously been used to cover walls. Although accustomed to decorative wall treatments, early American settlers could not afford imported wallpaper or decorated furniture. Traveling artisans roamed through the towns of New England hiring out their stenciling services. Coming back into fashion by the late 1970s, hand painted and stenciled designs have remained popular through current times.

Stenciling, paneling and striping effects can be created on walls, ceilings and floors. The paint application determines the contrast of the patterns, allowing the same design to be either soft or dramatic depending on the method of application. Hand embellishments by an artist can also lend a more custom look.

TO
SET THE
DRESSING
ROOM
apart from the
plastered master
bathroom, a subtle
stencil over plaster
makes the room
unique while
still relating to
the main area's
plastered walls.

THE
BEDROOM
WALLS,
stenciled
in a rich bronze
metallic, provide a
beautiful backdrop
for this dramatic
master retreat.

Designer - Betty Richter Arnold

THE DIOR BOUTIQUE

in Paris inspired this master closet that features a checkerboard design in gold and silver metallic paint topped with a gentle tea stain.

Opposite page, above: Trumeau mirror, sconces and daybed from Joyce Horn Antiques. Opposite page, below: Bed and console from George Cameron Nash. Bibliotheque from Carl Moore Antiques.

Hand painted paneling

in a variety of different methods adds a touch of
the unexpected, giving architectural interest to
rooms that otherwise have little composition.

*Right: French chair and lamp from Joyce Horn Antiques.
Reproduction French panel from Segreto Studios. Opposite page: Chandelier
from Antiques at Dunlavy. Chairs from Marburger Farm Antique Show.*

Designer - Lisa Dalton

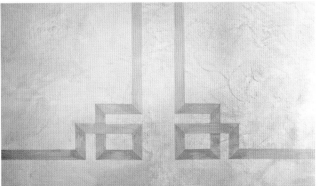

"I first saw a similar paneling technique
on a visit to France, and I just loved the
charm that it brought to the space."

Designers - Margie Slovack and Sarah Herndon
Building Design - Robert Dame Designs
Builder - Stonehenge Classic Homes, Inc.

"Implementing well done finishes is an art form, one that truly transforms a room and creates a mood. The textured gypsum plastered walls and ceilings of this stunning living room reflect the age of the reclaimed flooring, while providing a soft backdrop to the home's art and furnishings."

Resource
DIRECTORY

Designers & Consultants

Anne Lydick
713.828.3082
awli@usa.net

Betty Richter Arnold
832.630.1538
brarnold@tx.rr.com

Cindy Witmer
713.278.1919
www.cindywitmerdesigns.com

Cathy Carabello
Studio Bello, LP   713.501.6693
www.studiobellolp.com

Cherry Curlet
713.522.0742

Christen Bernard
713.857.8517
bernarddesign@sbcglobal.net

Don Connelly -AREA
713.668.1668
danielarea@sbcglobal.net

Donna Minyard
713.522.9700
dpminyard@gmail.com

Eleanor Cummings
713.962.2676
ebcummings@comcast.net

Ellie Bale
713.515.2664
ebale1@comcast.net

Ginger Barber
713.523.1925
www.gingerbarber.com

Jean Ellen Russell
713.467.2106
www.theaccessoryplace.com

John Kidd
713.961.1888
john@jkidd.net

Julia Blailock
713.622.8005
jmortonb@att.net

Julie Dodson
713.780.9200
www.dodsonanddaughter.com

Kara Childress
713.626.7948
kara@karachildressinc.com

Katie Galliano
713.306.3539
kgalliano@sbcglobal.net

Kate Scott
713.882.5995
scottkplace@aol.com

Lisa Dalton
713.806.5646
dalton1126@aol.com

Lisa McCollam
713.838.0212
lmccollamdesigns@sbcglobal.net

Maria Tracy
713.520.1312
www.tracy-design-studio.com

Marjorie Carter
603.876.4452

Nancy Sharp
713.857.8187
nasharp@att.net

Nicole Zarr
713.243.1963
nicole@triangleinteriors.com

Pamela Culpepper
713.501.5504
pmculpepper@yahoo.com

Rachael Miclette
Jacomini Miclette Design
713.524.8224

Rita Kissner
713.522.1062
kissner17@sbcglobal.net

Sandy Lucas
713.784.9423
www.lucaseilers.com

Sara Howell
sjhhowell@hotmail.com

Sarah West
713.417.6714
sarahwest.swa@gmail.com

Sheila Lyon
713.993.9001
sheila@sheilalyoninteriors.com

Slovack-Bass
Marjorie Slovack & Sarah Herndon
www.slovack-bass.com

Suzanne Duin
713.520.0342
suzanne@gbdesignonline.com

Tami Owen
713.515.0380
tamiowen@mac.com

Talbot Cooley
713.294.5506
tcinteriors@att.net

Teena Caldwell
281-980-2439
www.interiorsbyteena.com

Terry Harmon
713-557-8011
terrypharmon@gmail.com

Architects & building designers

Architectural Solutions, Inc.
Travis Mattingly   713.978.6989
tmattingly@asi-design.com

Charles W. Ligon AIA Architects
713.526.1288
Cligon3@sbcglobal.net

Colby Design
Rudy Colby 713.524.1497
www.colbydesign.net

Eubanks Group Architects
Ed Eubanks, Brandon Breaux
713.522.2652
www.eubanks-architects.com

Hollenbeck Architects, Inc.
713.529.5535
www.hollenbeckarchitects.com

J. Marshall Porterfield Jr.
713.526.4209

Michael T. Landrum Inc.
713.623.4605
michael@michaeltlandruminc.com

Murphy Mears Architects
713.529.9933
www.murphymears.com

Newberry Campa Architects, LLC
Ken Newberry   713.862.7992
www.newberrycampa.com

Robert Dame Designs
713.270.8225
www.robertdamedesigns.com

Rodney Stevens
713.489.9217

Shannon Sasser AIA
713.807.0550

Sullivan, Henry, Oggero & Assoc., Inc.   713.464.0740
www.shoplans.com

Tom Wilson & Associates
713.523.7451
tomwilsonarchitect.com

Villa Residential Design
713.961.4779
www.villaresidentialdesign.com

Builders

Abercrombie Builders Inc.
713.680.2424
andy@abuildersinc.com

Allan Edwards Builder
713.529.4481
www.aedwards.com

Barnett Custom Homes, Inc.
Pattie Barnett, 713.785.4475
pattibarnettbch@sbcglobal.net

Black Diamond Properties
713.532.8849
www.blackdiamondproperties.com

Builders West, Inc.
713.465.2233
www.builderswest.com

Corbel Custom Homes
713.461.6864

Crawford Renovations
713-463-8600
www.crghomes.com

Darryl Dieciedue
713.301.1999
dcicustombuilders@sbcglobal.net

David Levy
281-850-8092
levydr@sbcglobal.net

Elron Construction Inc
713.681.3222
www.elronconstruction.com

Epic Custom Homes
281.488.4927
epichomes@sbcglobal.net

Goodchild Builders
713.984.2272
www.goodchildbuilders.com

Iraj Taghi Custom Homes
713.961.0488
www.irajtaghihomes.com

Levitt Partnership
713.666.5311
hershlevitt@gmail.com

Memorial Builders Inc
713.266.6500

Michael Thurman Custom Homes
Sean Thurman   713.344.9262
www.mtcustomhomes.com

Mission Constructors, Inc.
713.523.9194
www.missionconstructors.com

Parker House Inc.
713.661.2685
www.parkerhousehouston.com

R.D. Allen Inc.
713.827.1292
www.rdallenbuilder.com

Roy Pruden LLC
713.349.8388
roypruden@sbcglobal.net

Richard Price Custom Homes
713.665.7711
www.richardpricecustomhomes.com

Southampton Group
713.528.0264
mbarone@flash.net

Steve Burns
713.784.1001
www.goodchildbuilders.com

Stonehenge Classic Homes, Inc.
David Crow   713.665.6530
www.stonehengeclassichomes.com

Thompson Custom Homes
832-327-0197
www.thompsoncustomhomes.com

University Towne Building Corporation
Dirk Hoyt, 713.840.8131
dhoyt@utbc.biz

Windham Builders
713.520.1605
www.windhambuilders.com

ANTIQUE DEALERS & TRADES

2 Lucy's
713.825.0045
www.2lucys.com

The Accessory Place
713-467-2106
www.theaccessoryplace.com

Designer - Christen Bernard
Architect - Eubanks Group Architects
Builder - Black Diamond Properties

291

Aidan Gray Home
www.aidangrayhome.com

Alamo Stone Company
1.800.501.0803
www.alamostonecompany.com

Alcon Lightcraft Co.
713.526.0680

Allan Knight and Assoc.
214.741.2227
www.allanknightasso.com

Allart Framing & Gallery
713.526.3631
www.allartframing.com

Andromeda
305.535.5767
www.andromedamurano.it

Annette Schatte Antiques
713.520.6546

Antiques at Dunlavy
713.942.1015

AR Floor Designs of Houston
281.932.9461
floordesignsofhouston@yahoo.com

Architectural Design Resource,
ADR   713.877.8366
www.adrhouston.com

Ardecora Fabric
George Cameron Nash-Houston
713-892-5710

AREA
713.668.1668
danielarea@sbcglobal.net

Arena Design
713.861.7630
www.arenadesign.us

Armani/Casa
212.339.5950
www.armanicasa.com

Bailey & Griffin
1.800.699.6554
www.baileygriffin.com

B. Berger Fabrics
713.599.0900

Bennison Fabrics
212.223.0373
www.bennisonfabrics.com

Bonhams & Butterfields
www.bonhams.com

Boxwood Interiors
713.528.1501

Britannia Antiques
713.529.3779

Brown
713.522.2151
www.shopbybrown.com

Brunschwig & Fils
914.684.5800
www.brunschwig.com

Cal Trevino
Master Craft Woodworks Inc.
713.923.6969

Cameron Collection
214.752.4421
www.cameroncollection.com

Canopy Designs Ltd.
www.canopydesigns.com

Canyon Marble & Granite
832.578.3113
canyon.marble.llc@sbcglobal.net

Canyon Mesquite
281.620.4468
www.canyonmesquite.com

Carl Moore Antiques
713.524.2502
www.carlmooreantiques.com

Carol Piper Rugs
713.524.2442
www.carolpiperrugs.com

Cavalier Fine Art
713.521.7711
www.cavalierfineart.com

Charles Thomas O'Neil
www.charlesthomasoneil.com

Charlotte Nail Antiques
713-869-9511
www.cninteriors.com

Chateau Domingue
713.961.3444
www.chateaudomingue.com

Christie's
www.christies.com

Christian Fischbacher
benu.fischbacher.com

Christina Karll
713.526.1101
www.christinakarll.com

Circa Lighting
713.526.4100
www.circalighting.com

Conrad Shades
www.conradshades.com

Cowtan & Tout
212.647.6900
www.cowtan.com

Creative Flooring Resources
713.522.1181

Currey & Company
www.curreycodealers.com

Custom Creations Furniture
800.268.6758
www.customcreationsfurniture.com

Custom Floors Unlimited
713.861.4139
www.customfloors.cc

David Sutherland Showroom
713.961.7886
www.davidsutherlandshowroom.com

Décor de Paris
800.221.6453
www.decordeparis.com

Dennis & Leen
310.652.0855
www.dennisandleen.com

Design House
713.803.4949
www.designhousetx.com

Dessin Fournir Companies
www.dessinfournir.com

Diana Hendrix
Represented by AREA
713-668-1668

Dick Wray
www.dickwrayartist.com

Donghia
www.donghia.com

Donna Phipps Stout
Valley House Gallery
www.valleyhouse.com

Duralee Fabrics
800.275.3872
www.duralee.com

Edward Ferrell
336.841.3028
www.ef-lm.com

Elegant Additions
713.522.0088
www.elegantadditions.net

Ellouise Abbott
713.626.5915
www.ellouiseabbott.com

Emmet Perry & Co.
713.961.4665
www.emmetperryrugandcarpet.com

Empire Antiques
713.629.5575

Etro
www.etro.it

Festoni
713.830.1077
www.festoni.com

Finnegan Gallery
312-738-9747
www.finnegangallery.com

Fireside Antiques
225.752.9565
www.firesideantiques.com

Florio Collection
www.floriocollection.com

For All Occasions
877.880.4333
www.faohouston.com

Formations
310.659.3062
www.formationsusa.com

Fortuny Fabric
Ellouise Abbot Showroom
www.ellouiseabbott.com

Found
713.522.9191
www.foundforthehome.com

Frame Tek Art Services
713.862.4747
www.theartframers.com

G&S Custom Draperies
713.464.9554
www.gandscustomdraperies.com

Gabriel Trevino
TrevCo
832.489.5275

George Cameron Nash
713-892-5710

Goravanchi Co. Persian Rugs
713.626.4200

Designer - Rachael Miclette
Architect - Eubanks Group Architects
Builder - Black Diamond Properties

Designer - Ellie Bale

International Granite & Marble Corp., IGM 713.690.1008
www.igmcorp.com

Iron Accents
866.438.4766
www.ironaccents.com

Jack Meier Gallery
713-526-2983
www.jackmeiergallery.com

Jackie Tileston
Holly Johnson Gallery
jtileston@gmail.com

Jacques Antiques
713.521.9026

Janet Wiebe Antiques
512.773.4499
www.janetwiebeantiques.com

Jas Gundry Antiques
713.524.6622
www.jasgundry.com

Joe Andoe
www.joeandoe.com

The Joseph Company
713.862.7490
www.josephcompany.com

Joseph Havel
www.artnet.com

Joyce Horn Antiques
713.688.0507
www.joycehornantiques.com

J. Roman Upholstery
713.665.1117

Julie Neill Designs
504.899.4201
www.julieneill.com

JVC Stoneworks
512.778.6033
www.jvcstoneworks.com

Karla Katz Antiques
504.897.0061

Keil's Antiques
www.keilsantiques.com

Kirby Antiques
713.520.1600
www.kirbyantiques.com

Koplavitch & Zimmer
www.koplavitchtextiles.com

Kravet
713.850.1461
www.kravet.com

Krispen
713.621.4404
www.krispenhome.com

Kuhl-Linscomb
713.526.6000
www.kuhl-linscomb.com

Lamani Designs
713.957.1635
www.lamani.com

Legacy Antiques
214.748.4606
www.legacyantiques.com

Designer - Kate Scott

Lee Jofa
713-629-5885
www.leejofa.com

Le Louvre French Antiques
214.742.2605
www.lelouvre-antiques.com

Leucos
732.225.0010
www.leucosusa.com

Leuders Limestone
325.228.4370
www.leuderslimestone.com

Lighting, Inc.
713.623.6500
www.lightinginc.com

Lighting Treasures
713.523.5267
www.lightingtreasures.com

Linda Dautreuil
www.lindadautreuil.com

Liz Spradling Antiques
713.526.1400
www.lizspradling.com

Longoria Collection
713.621.4241
www.longoriacollection.com

Louis J. Solomon
631.232.5300
www.louisjsolomon.com

Maison Maison
713.520.1654
www.maisonmaisonantiques.com

Marburger Farm Antique Show
800.999.2148
www.roundtop-marburger.com

Marc Anthony Rugs
713.861.3000
www.marcanthonyrugs.com

Marge Carson
www.margecarson.com

Marvic Textiles
www.marvictextiles.co.uk

Master Tile
888.388.2842
www.mastertilesales.com

Materials Marketing
713.960.8601
www.mstoneandtile.com

Matt Camron Rugs & Tapestries
713.528.2666
www.mattcamron.com

Mecox Gardens
713.355.2103
www.mecoxgardens.com

Memorial Antiques & Interiors,
MAI   713.827.8087
www.maihouston.com

Metal Railing of America, Inc.
713.957.3023

The Mews
214.748.9070
www.mewsantiques.com

Michael Aram
www.michaelaram.com

Michel Alexis
Stephen Haller Gallery
www.stephenhallergallery.com

Michelle Y. Williams
713-521-7701
www.michelleywilliams.com

Minton-Spidell Incorporated
310.836.0403
www.minton-spidell.com

M & M Carpet
713.621.1556
www.mandmcarpet.com

Morrison Supply Company
817.870.2227
www.morsco.com

Muniz Plastics
305.634.8848
www.munizplastics.com

Nancy Corzine
312.645.4500
www.nancycorzine.com

Neal & Co. Upholstery
713.956.7100

Nouri Gallery
713.528.8008
www.nouri.com

Oriental Rug Gallery of Texas
713.622.0647
www.orgtx.com

Olympus Marble & Granite
713.827.8700

Panache Lighting
www.panachelighting.com

Perennials Outdoor Fabrics
www.perennialsfabrics.com
214.638.4162

Peter Fasano
413.528.6872
www.peterfasano.com

Pettigrew Associates
www.pettigrew-usa.com

Pindler & Pindler
www.pindler.com

The Pittet Company
214.748.8999
www.pittetco.com

Plush Home
713.522.5230
www.plushhome.net

Pride Of Persia Rug Co.
713-522-7870
www.prideofpersia.com

Restoration Hardware
www.restorationhardware.com

Rob Reasoner
McClain Gallery
www.mcclaingallery.com

Robert Allen/Beacon Hill
713-439-0200
www.robertallendesign.com

Rogers & Goffigon
George Cameron Nash
713-892-5710

Rose Tarlow Melrose House
323.651.2202
www.rosetarlow.com

R.W. Taylor, Inc.
www.rwtaylorinc.com

Samuel & Sons
212.704.8000
www.samuelandsons.com

San Jacinto Stone
713.868.3466

Scalamandre
713.627.8315
www.scalamandre.com

Schenck & Company
713.266.7608
www.schenckandcompany.com

Secrets of Segreto Blog
www.segretosecrets.squarespace.com

Segreto Finishes
Leslie Sinclair   713.461.5210
www.segretofinishes.com

Segreto Studios
  Allan Rodewald
  Kiah Denson
  Leslie Sinclair
  Rachel Schwind
713.461.5210
www.segretostudios.net

Shabby Slips
713.630.0066
www.shabbyslipshouston.com

Sherle Wagner
713-871-1608
www.sherlewagner.com

Signoria Firenze
www.signoria.com

Silkworks
510.839.7022
www.silkworkstextiles.com

Stark Fabric
713.623.4034
www.old-world-weavers.com

Tara Shaw
713.533.9744
www.tarashaw.com

Travers & Co.
George Cameron Nash
713-892-5710

Togar Rugs
828.687.1968
www.togarrugs.com

Topstitch, Inc.
713.803.9330
7026 Old Katy Road #163

Twenty Six Twenty
713.840.9877
www.twentysixtwenty.com

Vervain
1.800.611.8686
www.vervain.com

Vieux Interiors
713.626.9500
www.vieuxinteriors.com

Visual Comfort & Co.
713.686.5999
www.visualcomfort.com

Walker Zanger
713.880.9292
www.walkerzanger.com

Walter Lee Culp & Assoc.
713-623-4670
www.culpassociates.com

Watkins Culver Antiques
713.528.1608
www.watkinsculver.com

Waterworks
1.800.899.6757
www.waterworks.com

Westheimer Plumbing
& Hardware 713.942.9519
www.westheimerplumbing.com

W. Gardner, Ltd.
713.521.1027
www.wgardnerltd.com

Wirthmore Antiques
504.269.0660
www.wirthmoreantiques.com

The Woodshop of Texas
888.950.9663
www.woodshopoftexas.com

Zoffany
www.zoffany.com

Design & PHOTOGRAPHY

PHOTO CREDITS

Wade Blissard, Principal Photographer
with the exception of the following images:

David Schilling Photography
Pages 128, 131-133, 208-211, 214-218, 220-223, 267 bottom right, 278 bottom right

Janet Lenzen Photography
Pages 166-171, 267 top left

Baxter Imaging LLC
Pages 38-46

Jack Thompson Photography
Page 263

Stacey Parrish-Collins
Page 300 and back flap

James Farmer
Page 250

TK Images
Page 291

©All photographs are the copyright of the artists.

Wade Blissard
281.250.4425
www.shooterwade.com

David Schilling Photography
www.schillingphoto.com

Baxter Imaging LLC
Michael Baxter
www.baxterimaging.com

Janet Lenzen Photography
713.703.9656
lenzenjml@yahoo.com

James Farmer
713-398-7657

Jack Thompson Photography
713.256.6184
lucky35@mac.com

Stacey Parrish-Collins
staceyc@rowanandlucky.com
www.rowanandlucky.com

TK Images
713.545.9177
www.tkimages.com

GRAPHIC DESIGN

Muffy Buvens, Graphic Design & Layout
mbuvens@gmail.com
713.419.6101

THIS BOOK IS DEDICATED TO

the wonderful homeowners, designers, builders and architects with whom I have worked,
my Segreto Finishes team and my family, John, Matthew, Kirby and Sammy.
Without each of you, this book and my career would not be possible. - *L. S.*